GW00357261

THE DIFFICULT
DOCTRINE OF THE
LOVE OF GOD

THE DIFFICULT
DOCTRINE OF THE
LOVE OF GOD

D. A. CARSON

Inter-Varsity Press

INTER-VARSITY PRESS
38 De Montfort Street, Leicester LE1 7GP, England
Email: ivp@uccf.org.uk
Website: www.ivpbooks.com

© 2000 by D. A. Carson

All rights reserved. No part of this publication may be reproduced,
stored in a retrieval system, or transmitted, in any form or by any
means, electronic, mechanical, photocopying, recording or
otherwise, without the prior permission of the publisher or the
Copyright Licensing Agency.

Unless otherwise stated, Scripture quotations in this publication are
from the Holy Bible, New International Version. Copyright
© 1973, 1978, 1984 by International Bible Society. Used by
permission of Hodder and Stoughton, a division of Hodder Headline
Ltd. All rights reserved. 'NIV' is a registered trademark of
International Bible Society. UK trademark number 1448790.

Published by arrangement with Crossway Books, a division of Good
News Publishers, 1300 Crescent Street, Wheaton, Illinois 60187, USA.

First British edition 2000
Reprinted 2000, 2001, 2003, 2004

British Library Cataloguing-in-publication Data
A catalogue record for this book is available from the British Library.

ISBN 0-85111-975-1

Set in Garamond
Typeset in Great Britain

Printed and bound in Great Britain by Cox & Wyman Ltd, Reading,
Berkshire

*Inter-Varsity Press is the publishing division of the Universities and
Colleges Christian Fellowship (formerly the Inter-Varsity Fellowship),
a student movement linking Christian Unions in universities and
colleges throughout Great Britain, and a member movement of the
International Fellowship of Evangelical Students. For more
information about local and national activities write to UCCF,
38 De Montfort Street, Leicester LE1 7GP, email us at
email@uccf.org.uk or visit the UCCF website at www.uccf.org.uk*

Contents

Preface

Although parts of this book were first delivered as
lectures in various places, the four chapters, more or
less as printed here, were prepared in the first instance
as the W. H. Griffith Thomas Lectures and were
delivered at Dallas Theological Seminary in February
1998.

I am very grateful for the many kindnesses shown
me during the four days of my visit. Faculty members
went out of their way to be welcoming. It was good to
renew old acquaintances and friendships and to
establish new ones. The academic dean, Dr Mark
Bailey, and his staff were solicitous and helpful beyond
mere professionalism.

Since then I have repeated the four lectures, each
time lightly revised, at Carey Baptist College in New
Zealand, Moore Theological College in Sydney,

Australia, and at Gilcomston Church in Aberdeen. In each case I benefited from both the hospitality and the questions.

I am especially grateful to God for the opportunity afforded by these lectures to put into print a little theological reflection that has occupied me for some time. The theme of the love of God is not soon exhausted either in our experience or in our theology. Doubtless it will occupy our reflection and call forth our adoration in eternity. This little book makes no pretence to either comprehensiveness or profundity. It is not much more than a priming of the pump. In part it covers ground that many Christians three centuries' ago knew something about, things widely lost today. If this book makes even a small contribution to their recovery, I shall be grateful.

The lectures first appeared in print in the four fascicles of the 1999 volume of *Bibliotheca Sacra*. I am grateful to Crossway Books, USA, and IVP, UK, for producing the lectures in this form, slightly revised yet again, thereby making them more widely available. It will soon be obvious to the reader that, with minor exceptions, I have retained the relative informality of the lecture rather than turn these chapters into essays. Also I would very much like to thank my graduate assistant, Sigurd Grindheim, for compiling the indexes.

Soli Deo gloria.

D. A. Carson
Trinity Evangelical Divinity School

1
On distorting
the love of God

On learning the title of this series, 'The difficult doctrine of the love of God', you might well be forgiven for thinking that the 1998 W. H. Griffith Thomas lecturer has taken leave of his senses. If he had chosen to speak on 'The difficult doctrine of the Trinity', or 'The difficult doctrine of predestination', at least his title would have been coherent. But isn't the doctrine of the love of God, well, *easy* compared with such high-flown and mysterious teachings?

Why the doctrine of the love of God must be judged difficult

There are at least five reasons.

(1) If people believe in God at all today, the overwhelming majority hold that this God –

however he, she, or it may be understood – is a loving being. But that is what makes the task of the Christian witness so daunting. For this widely disseminated belief in the love of God is set with increasing frequency in some matrix other than biblical theology. The result is that when informed Christians talk about the love of God, they mean something very different from what is meant in the surrounding culture. Worse, neither side may perceive that that is the case.

Consider some recent products of the film industry, that celluloid preserve that both reflects and shapes Western culture. For our purposes science-fiction films may be divided into two kinds. Perhaps the more popular ones are the slam-bang, shoot-'em-up kind, such as *Independence Day* or the four-part *Alien* series, complete with loathsome evil. Obviously the aliens have to be nasty, or there would be no threat and therefore no targets and no fun. Rarely do these films set out to convey a cosmological message, still less a spiritual one.

The other sort of film in this class, trying to convey a message even as it seeks to entertain, almost always portrays the ultimate power as benevolent. On the border between the two kinds of films is the *Star Wars* series, with its treatment of the morally ambiguous Force, but even this series tilts toward the assumption of a final victory for the 'light' side of the Force. *ET*, as Roy Anker has put it, is 'a glowing-heart incarnation tale that climaxes in resurrection and ascension'.[1] And now in Jodie Foster's *Contact*, the unexplained intelligence is suffused with love, wisely provident, gently awesome.

Anker himself thinks this 'indirection', as he calls it, is a great help to the Christian cause. Like the writings of J. R. R. Tolkien and C. S. Lewis, these films help people *indirectly* to appreciate the sheer goodness and love of God. I am not nearly so sanguine. Tolkien and Lewis still lived in a world shaped by the Judeo-Christian heritage. Their 'indirection' was read by others in the culture who had also been shaped by that heritage, even though many of their readers were not Christians in any biblical sense.

But the worldview of *Contact* is monistic, naturalistic, pluralistic (after all, the film was dedicated to Carl Sagan). It has far more connections with New Age, Pollyannaish optimism than anything substantive. Suddenly the Christian doctrine of the love of God becomes very difficult, for the entire framework in which it is set in Scripture has been replaced.

(2) To put this another way, we live in a culture in which many other and complementary truths about God are widely *dis*believed. I do not think that what the Bible says about the love of God can long survive at the forefront of our thinking if it is abstracted from the sovereignty of God, the holiness of God, the wrath of God, the providence of God, or the personhood of God – to mention only a few non-negotiable elements of basic Christianity.

The result, of course, is that the love of God in our culture has been purged of anything the culture finds uncomfortable. The love of God has been

sanitized, democratized, and above all sentimentalized. This process has been going on for some time.
My generation was taught to sing, 'What the world
needs now is love, sweet love', in which we robustly
instruct the Almighty that we do not need another
mountain (we have enough of them), but we could
do with some more love. The hubris is staggering.

It has not always been so. In generations when
almost everyone believed in the justice of God,
people sometimes found it difficult to believe in the
love of God. The preaching of the love of God came
as wonderful good news. Nowadays if you tell people
that God loves them, they are unlikely to be
surprised. Of course God loves me; he's like that,
isn't he? Besides, why shouldn't he love me? I'm kind
of cute, or at least as nice as the next person. I'm
okay, you're okay, and God loves you and me.

Even in the mid-1980s, according to Andrew
Greeley, three-quarters of his respondents in an
important poll reported that they preferred to think
of God as 'friend' than as 'king'.[2] I wonder what the
percentage would have been if the option had been
'friend' or 'judge'. Today most people seem to have
little difficulty believing in the love of God; they
have far more difficulty believing in the justice of
God, the wrath of God, and the non-contradictory
truthfulness of an omniscient God. But is the
biblical teaching on the love of God maintaining its
shape when the meaning of 'God' dissolves in mist?

We must not think that Christians are immune
from these influences. In an important book, Marsha
Witten surveys what is being preached in the

Protestant pulpit.[3] Let us admit the limitations of her study. Her pool of sermons was drawn, on the one hand, from the Presbyterian Church (USA), scarcely a bastion of confessional evangelicalism; and, on the other, from churches belonging to the Southern Baptist Convention. Strikingly, on many of the crucial issues, there was only marginal statistical difference between these two ecclesiastical heritages. A more significant limitation was that the sermons she studied all focused on the parable of the prodigal son (Luke 15). That is bound to slant sermons in a certain direction.

Nevertheless her book abounds in lengthy quotations from these sermons, and they are immensely troubling. There is a powerful tendency 'to present God through characterizations of his inner states, with an emphasis on his emotions, which closely resemble those of human beings ... God is more likely to "feel" than to "act," to "think" than to "say."'[4] Or again:

> The relatively weak notion of God's fearsome capabilities regarding judgment is underscored by an almost complete lack of discursive construction of anxiety around one's future state. As we have already seen, the sermons dramatize feelings of anxiety for listeners over many other (this-worldly) aspects of their removal from God, whether they are discussing in the vocabulary of sin or in other formulations. But even when directly referring to the unconverted, only two sermons press on

fear of God's judgment by depicting anxiety over salvation, and each text does this only obliquely, as it makes the point indirectly on its way to other issues while buffering the audience from negative feelings ... The transcendent, majestic, awesome God of Luther and Calvin – whose image informed early Protestant visions of the relationship between human beings and the divine – has undergone a softening of demeanor through the American experience of Protestantism, with only minor exceptions ... Many of the sermons depict a God whose behavior is regular, patterned, and predictable; he is portrayed in terms of the consistency of his behavior, of the conformity of his actions to the single rule of 'love.'[5]

With such sentimentalizing of God multiplying in Protestant churches, it does not take much to see how difficult maintaining a *biblical* doctrine of the love of God can be.

(3) Some elements of the larger and still developing patterns of postmodernism play into the problem with which we are dealing. Because of remarkable shifts in the West's epistemology, more and more people believe that the only heresy left is the view that there is such a thing as heresy. They hold that all religions are fundamentally the same and that, therefore, it is not only rude but profoundly ignorant and old-fashioned to try to win others to your beliefs, since implicitly that is

announcing that theirs are inferior.[6]

This stance, fuelled in the West, now reaches into many parts of the world. For example, in a recent book Caleb Oluremi Oladipo outlines *The Development of the Doctrine of the Holy Spirit in the Yoruba (African) Indigenous Church Movement.*[7] His concern is to show the interplay between Christian beliefs and Yoruba traditional religion on the indigenous church. After establishing 'two distinct perspectives' that need not detain us here, Oladipo writes:

> These two paradigmic [*sic*] perspectives in the book are founded on a fundamental assertion that the nature of God is universal love. This assertion presupposes that while Western missionaries asserted that the nature of God is universal love, most missionaries have denied salvation to various portions of the world population, and in most cases they did so indiscriminately. The book points out the inconsistencies of such a view, and attempts to bring coherency between Christianity and other religions in general, and Yoruba Traditional Religion in particular.[8]

In short, the most energetic cultural tide, postmodernism, powerfully reinforces the most sentimental, syncretistic, and often pluralistic views of the love of God, with no other authority base than the postmodern epistemology itself. But that makes the articulation of a biblical doctrine of God and of a biblical doctrine of the love of God an extraordinarily difficult challenge.

(4) The first three difficulties stem from developments in the culture that make grasping and articulating the doctrine of the love of God a considerable challenge. This fourth element is in certain respects more fundamental. In the cultural rush toward a sentimentalized, sometimes even non-theistic vision of the love of God, we Christians have sometimes been swept along to the extent that we have forgotten that *within Christian confessionalism* the doctrine of the love of God poses its difficulties. This side of two world wars; genocide in Russia, China, Europe, and Africa; mass starvation; Hitler and Pol Pot; endless disgusting corruptions at home and abroad – all in recent history – is the love of God such an obvious doctrine? Of course that is raising the difficulties from an experiential point of view. One may do the same thing from the perspective of systematic theology. Precisely how does one integrate what the Bible says about the love of God with what the Bible says about God's sovereignty, extending as it does even over the domain of evil? What does love mean in a Being whom at least some texts treat as impassible? How is God's love tied to God's justice?

In other words, one of the most dangerous results of the impact of contemporary sentimentalized versions of love on the church is our widespread inability to think through the fundamental questions that alone enable us to maintain a doctrine of God in biblical proportion and balance. However glorious and privileged a task that may be, none of it is easy.

We are dealing with God, and fatuous reductionisms are bound to be skewed and dangerous.

(5) Finally, the doctrine of the love of God is sometimes portrayed within Christian circles as much easier and more obvious than it really is, and this is achieved by overlooking some of the distinctions the Bible itself introduces when it depicts the love of God. This is so important that it becomes my next major point.

Some different ways the Bible speaks of the love of God

I had better warn you that not all of the passages to which I refer actually use the word *love*. When I speak of the doctrine of the love of God, I include themes and texts that depict God's love without ever using the word, just as Jesus tells parables that depict grace without using that word.

With that warning to the fore, I draw your attention to five distinguishable ways the Bible speaks of the love of God. This is not an exhaustive list, but it is heuristically useful.

(1) *The peculiar love of the Father for the Son, and of the Son for the Father.* John's Gospel is especially rich in this theme. Twice we are told that the Father loves the Son, once with the verb *agapaō* (John 3:35), and once with *phileō* (John 5:20). Yet the evangelist also insists that the world must learn that Jesus loves the Father (John 14:31). This intra-Trinitarian love of God not only marks off Christian monotheism from all other monotheisms, but is

bound up in surprising ways with revelation and redemption. I shall return to this theme in the next chapter.

(2) *God's providential love over all that he has made.* By and large the Bible veers away from using the word *love* in this connection, but the theme is not hard to find. God creates everything, and before there is a whiff of sin, he pronounces all that he has made to be 'good' (Gen. 1 – 2). This is the product of a *loving* Creator. The Lord Jesus depicts a world in which God clothes the grass of the fields with the glory of wild flowers seen by no human being, perhaps, but seen by God. The lion roars and hauls down its prey, but it is God who feeds the animal. The birds of the air find food, but that is the result of God's loving providence, and not a sparrow falls from the sky apart from the sanction of the Almighty (Matt. 6:26; 10:29). If this were not a benevolent providence, a *loving* providence, then the moral lesson that Jesus drives home, viz. that this God can be trusted to provide for his own people, would be incoherent.

(3) *God's salvific stance toward his fallen world.* God so loved *the world* that he gave his Son (John 3:16). I know that some try to take *kosmos* ('world') here to refer to the elect. But that really will not do. All the evidence of the usage of the word in John's Gospel is against the suggestion. True, *world* in John does not so much refer to bigness as to badness. In John's vocabulary, *world* is primarily the moral order in wilful and culpable rebellion against God. In John 3:16 God's love in sending the Lord Jesus is to be

admired not because it is extended to so big a thing as the world, but to so bad a thing; not to so many people, as to such wicked people. Nevertheless elsewhere John can speak of 'the *whole* world' (1 John 2:2), thus bringing bigness and badness together. More importantly, in Johannine theology the disciples themselves once belonged to the world but were drawn out of it (e.g., John 15:19). On this axis, God's love for the world cannot be collapsed into his love for the elect.

The same lesson is learned from many passages and themes in Scripture. However much God stands in judgment over the world, he also presents himself as the God who invites and commands all human beings to repent. He orders his people to carry the gospel to the farthest corner of the world, proclaiming it to men and women everywhere. To rebels the sovereign Lord calls out, 'As surely as I live ... I take no pleasure in the death of the wicked, but rather that they turn from their ways and live. Turn! Turn from your evil ways! Why will you die, O house of Israel?' (Ezek. 33:11).[9]

(4) *God's particular, effective, selecting love toward his elect.* The elect may be the entire nation of Israel, or the church as a body or individuals. In each case, God sets his affection on his chosen ones in a way in which he does not set his affection on others. The people of Israel are told, 'The LORD did not set his affection on you and choose you because you were more numerous than other peoples, for you were the fewest of all peoples. But it was because the LORD loved you and kept the oath he swore to your

forefathers that he brought you out with a mighty hand and redeemed you from the land of slavery, from the power of Pharaoh king of Egypt' (Deut. 7:7–8; cf. 4:37). Again: 'To the LORD your God belong the heavens, even the highest heavens, the earth and everything in it. Yet the LORD set his affection on your forefathers and loved them, and he chose you, their descendants, above all the nations, as it is today' (10:14–15).

The striking thing about these passages is that when Israel is contrasted with the universe or with other nations, the distinguishing feature has nothing of personal or national merit; it is nothing other than the love of God. In the very nature of the case, then, God's love is directed toward Israel in these passages in a way in which it is *not* directed toward other nations.

Obviously, this way of speaking of the love of God is unlike the other three ways of speaking of God's love that we have looked at so far. This discriminating feature of God's love surfaces frequently. 'I have loved Jacob, but Esau I have hated' (Mal. 1:2–3), God declares. Allow all the room you like for the Semitic nature of this contrast, observing that the absolute form can be a way of articulating absolute preference; yet the fact is that God's love in such passages is peculiarly directed toward the elect.

Similarly in the New Testament: Christ 'loved the church' (Eph. 5:25). Repeatedly the New Testament texts tell us that the love of God or the love of Christ is directed toward those who constitute the church.

To this subject I will return in the fourth chapter.

(5) *Finally, God's love is sometimes said to be directed toward his own people in a provisional or conditional way – conditional, that is, on obedience.* It is part of the relational structure of knowing God; it does not have to do with how we become true followers of the living God, but with our relationship with him once we do know him. 'Keep yourselves in God's love,' Jude exhorts his readers (v. 21), leaving the unmistakable impression that someone might *not* keep himself or herself in the love of God. Clearly this is not God's providential love; it is pretty difficult to escape that. Nor is this God's yearning love, reflecting his salvific stance toward our fallen race. Nor is it his eternal, elective love. If words mean anything, one does not, as we shall see, walk away from that love either.

Jude is not the only one who speaks in such terms. The Lord Jesus commands his disciples to remain in his love (John 15:9), and adds, 'If you obey my commands, you will remain in my love, just as I have obeyed my Father's commands and remain in his love' (John 15:10). To draw a feeble analogy: although there is a sense in which my love for my children is immutable, so help me God, regardless of what they do, there is another sense in which they know well enough that they must remain in my love. If for no good reason my teenagers do not get home by the time I have prescribed, the least they will experience is a loud telling off, and they may come under some restrictive sanctions. There is no use reminding them that I am doing this because I love them. That is true, but the manifestation of my love for them when I ground them and when I take them out for a meal or attend one of their concerts or take my son fishing or my daughter on an excursion of some sort is rather different in the two cases. Only the latter will feel much more like remaining in my love than falling under my wrath.

Nor is this a phenomenon of the new covenant alone. The Decalogue declares God to be the one who shows his love 'to a thousand generations *of those who love me and keep my commandments*' (Exod. 20:6). Yes, 'The LORD is compassionate and gracious, slow to anger, abounding in love' (Ps. 103:8). In this context, his love is *set over against* his wrath. Unlike some other texts we shall examine, his people live under his love *or* under his wrath, in function of their covenantal faithfulness: 'He will not *always* accuse, nor will he harbour his anger for ever; he does not treat us as our sins deserve or repay us according to our iniquities. For as high as the heavens are above the earth, so great is his love *for those who fear him* ... As a father has compassion on his children, so the LORD has compassion *on those who fear him* ... But from everlasting to everlasting the LORD's love is *with those who fear him* ... *with those who keep his covenant and remember to obey his precepts*' (Ps. 103:9–11, 13, 17–18). This is the language of relationship between God and the covenant community.

I shall conclude this chapter with:

Three preliminary observations on these distinctive ways of talking about the love of God

These three reflections will be teased out a little more in the remaining chapters. Nevertheless it will be useful to draw some strands together.

(1) It is easy to see what will happen if any one of these five biblical ways of talking about the love of God is absolutized and made exclusive, or made the controlling grid by which the other ways of talking about the love of God are relativized.

If we begin with the intra-Trinitarian love of God and use that as the model for all of God's loving relationships, we shall fail to observe the distinctions that must be maintained. The love of the Father for the Son and the love of the Son for the Father are expressed in a relationship of perfection, untarnished by sin on either side. However much the intra-Trinitarian love serves, as we shall see, as a model of the love to be exchanged between Jesus and his followers, there is no sense in which the love of the Father redeems the Son, or the love of the Son is expressed in a relationship of forgiveness granted and received. As precious, indeed as properly awesome, as the intra-Trinitarian love of God is, an exclusive focus in this direction takes too little account of how God manifests himself toward his rebellious image-bearers in wrath, in love, in the cross.

If the love of God is nothing more than his providential ordering of everything, we are not far from a beneficent if somewhat mysterious 'force'. It would be easy to integrate that kind of stance into pantheism or some other form of monism. Deep-green environmentalism may thereby be strengthened, but not the grand story-line that takes us from creation to new creation to new heaven and new earth, by way of the cross and resurrection of our Master.

If the love of God is exclusively portrayed as an inviting, yearning, sinner-seeking, rather lovesick passion, we may strengthen the hands of Arminians, semi-Pelagians, Pelagians, and those more interested in God's inner emotional life than in his justice and glory, but the cost will be massive. There is some truth in this picture of God, as we shall see; some glorious truth. Made absolute, however, it not only treats complementary texts as if they were not there, but it steals God's sovereignty from him and our security from us. It espouses a theology of grace rather different from Paul's theology of grace, and at its worst ends up with a God so insipid he can neither intervene to save us nor deploy his chastening rod against us. His love is too 'unconditional' for that. This is a world far removed from the pages of Scripture.

If the love of God refers exclusively to his love for the elect, it is easy to drift toward a simple and absolute bifurcation: God loves the elect and hates the reprobate. Rightly positioned, there is truth in this assertion; stripped of complementary biblical truths, that same assertion has engendered hyper-Calvinism. I use the term advisedly, referring to groups within the Reformed tradition that have forbidden the free offer of the gospel. Spurgeon fought them in his day.[10] Their number is not great today, but their echoes are found in young Reformed ministers who know it is right to offer the gospel freely, but who have no idea how to do it without contravening some element in their conception of Reformed theology.[11]

If the love of God is construed entirely within the kind of discourse that ties God's love to our obedience (e.g., 'Keep yourselves in the love of God'), the dangers threatening us change once again. True, in a church characterized rather more by personal preference and antinomianism than by godly fear of the Lord, such passages surely have something to say to us. But divorced from complementary biblical utterances about the love of God, such texts may drive us backwards toward merit theology, endless fretting about whether or not we have been good enough today to enjoy the love of God – to be free from all the paroxysms of guilt from which the cross alone may free us.

In short, we need *all* of what Scripture says on this subject, or the doctrinal and pastoral ramifications will prove disastrous.

(2) We must not view these ways of talking about the love of God as independent, compartmentalized, *loves* of God. It will not help to begin talking too often about God's providential love, his elective love, his intra-Trinitarian love, and so forth, as if each were hermetically sealed off from the other. Nor can we allow any one of these ways of talking about the

love of God to be diminished by the others, even as we cannot, on scriptural evidence, allow any one of them to domesticate all the others. God is God, and he is one. Not only must we gratefully acknowledge that God in the perfection of his wisdom has thought it best to provide us with these various ways of talking of his love if we are to think of him aright, but we must hold these truths together and learn to integrate them in biblical proportion and balance. We must apply them to our lives and to the lives of those to whom we minister, with insight and sensitivity shaped by the way these truths function in Scripture.

(3) Within the framework established so far, we may well ask ourselves how well certain evangelical clichés stand up.

(a) 'God's love is unconditional.' Doubtless that is true in the fourth sense, with respect to God's elective love. But it is certainly not true in the fifth sense: God's discipline of his children means that he may turn upon us with the divine equivalent of the 'wrath' of a parent on a wayward teenager. Indeed, to cite the cliché 'God's love is unconditional' to a Christian who is drifting toward sin may convey the wrong impression and do a lot of damage. Such Christians need to be told that they will remain in God's love only if they do what he says. Obviously, then, it is pastorally important to know what passages and themes to apply to which people at any given time.

(b) 'God loves everyone exactly the same way.' That is certainly true in passages belonging to the second category, in the domain of providence. After all, God sends his sunshine and his rain upon the just and the unjust alike. But it is certainly not true in passages belonging to the fourth category, the domain of election.

One or two more clichés will be probed later in these chapters. Already, however, it is clear that what the Bible says about the love of God is more complex and nuanced than what is allowed by mere slogan-eering.

To sum up: Christian faithfulness entails our responsibility to grow in our grasp of what it means to confess that God is love. To this end we devote the remaining chapters.

2

God is love

'God is love,' John writes in his first letter (4:8, 16). The biblical writers treat the love of God as a wonderful thing, wholly admirable and praiseworthy, even surprising when the objects of his love are rebellious human beings. But what does the predication 'God is love' actually mean?

We might first ask how we shall find out. An older generation might have attempted to answer the question primarily through word studies. Especially prominent was the attempt to invest the *agapaō* word group with theological weight.

I have discussed some of these matters elsewhere and must not repeat myself too much here. Still, my book *Exegetical Fallacies*[1] may not have been inflicted upon you, and the point I wish to make is sufficiently important that repetition will do no harm.

How not to proceed

In the past many have tried to assign the love of God and, derivatively, Christian love to one particular word group. The classic treatment is that of Anders Nygren.[2] The noun *erōs* (not found in the New Testament) refers to sexual love, erotic love; the *phileō* word group refers to emotional love, the love of friendship and feeling. By contrast, the *agapaō* word group refers to willed love, an act of willed self-sacrifice for the good of another. It has no necessary emotional component, however generous it may be. Moreover, it was argued, the reason the *agapaō* word group became extremely popular in the Septuagint and subsequently in the New Testament is that writers in the biblical tradition realized they needed some word other than those currently available to convey the glorious substance of the love of the God of Judeo-Christian revelation; so they deployed this extremely rare word group and filled it with the content just described, until it triumphed in frequency as well as in substance.

Whether or not this is a fair description of divine love, we shall examine in due course. What is now quite clear to almost everyone who works in the fields of linguistics and semantics is that such an understanding of love cannot be tied in any univocal way to the *agapaō* word group. Let me briefly list the most important reasons.

(1) Careful diachronic work has been done on Greek words for 'love'.[3] In the pre-classical Greek tradition, there was a homonymic clash between two

verbs – *kyneō*, 'to kiss', and *kynō*, 'to impregnate'. Certain forms of the two verbs are identical, e.g., the aorist *ekysa*. Inevitably, this gave rise to many salacious puns, which forced *kyneō* into obsolescence, replaced by *phileō* (which is used, for instance, when Judas kisses Jesus, Luke 22:47). This meant, of course, that *phileō* could be taken to mean 'to kiss' or 'to love', which in the Attic period encouraged the rise of other words for 'to love'. By the end of that period and the beginning of the Hellenistic era, the verb *agapaō* was one of those verbs, though there is not yet any evidence of the cognate noun *agapē*. In other words, there are excellent diachronic reasons in Greek philology to explain the rise of the *agapaō* word group, so one should not rush too quickly toward theological explanations.

(2) Even within the Septuagint Old Testament, it is far from clear that the *agapaō* word group always refers to some 'higher' or more noble or less emotional form of love. For example, in 2 Samuel 13 (LXX), Amnon incestuously rapes his half-sister Tamar. He 'loves' her, we are told. His deed is a vicious act, transparently sexual, emotional, and violent – and both *agapaō* and *phileō* are used.

(3) In the Gospel of John, as I mentioned in the first chapter, twice we are told that the Father 'loves' the Son (3:35; 5:20). The first time the verb is *agapaō*, while the second it is *phileō*. It is impossible to detect any difference in meaning. Surely it is not that God is more emotional in the second instance than in the first. When Paul writes that Demas has deserted him because he 'loved' this present evil

world (2 Tim. 4:10), the verb the apostle chooses is *agapaō* – an incongruous choice if it refers to willed self-denial for the sake of the other.

(4) Occasionally someone argues that a distinction must be maintained between the two verbs because, however synonymous they may be in many occurrences, inevitably there is a little semantic overhang – i.e., one or the other will be used on occasions where the other one could not be. As we have seen, *phileō* can mean 'to kiss'; *agapaō* never has this meaning. Kissing is part of the semantic overhang of *phileō*. This means that in any context there is always a subtle distinction to be made between the two verbs, since the total semantic range of the two is not the same in each case. But although this is a valid argument for the *lexical* meaning of the two verbs, it has no bearing on any concrete passage. This is to fall into the trap of what linguists call 'illegitimate totality transfer' – the illegitimate importing of the *entire* semantic range of a word into that word in a particular context.

(5) The best English example is simply the verb *love*. One may use it for sexual intercourse, platonic love, emotional love, the love of God, and more. The context defines and delimits the word, precisely as it does the verbs for 'love' in the pages of holy Scripture.

(6) So far as Christian love is concerned, one observes that in 1 Corinthians 13 *agapē* cannot be reduced to willed altruism. Even believers who give their bodies to be burned or who give all they have to feed the poor – both willed acts of self-denial for

the sake of others — may do so *without* love, and according to the apostle it profits them nothing. The least one must conclude from this is that Christian love cannot be reduced to willed altruism.

(7) Although I have never traced it out in detail, I suspect that the heritage of understanding *agapaō* to refer to a willed love independent of emotion and committed to the other's good has been influenced by the schoolmen and other philosophical theologians of a bygone era, who denied there was feeling in God. To have feeling, they argued, would imply passivity, i.e., a susceptibility to impression from people or events outside himself, and this is surely incompatible with the very nature of God. Thus God's love must be fundamentally different from ours. The only point of similarity between God's love and our love, they argued, is self-communication; it is not emotion or feeling. Counter-evidence found in the Bible (and there is a lot of it!) must then be marginalized by dismissing it as anthropopathism (the emotional counterpoint to anthropomorphism). More than a century ago, Charles Hodge responded:

> Here again we have to choose between a mere philosophical speculation and the clear testimony of the Bible, and of our own moral and religious nature. Love of necessity involves feeling, and if there be no feeling in God, there can be no love ... The philosophical objection against ascribing feeling to God bears ... with equal force against the ascription to Him of knowledge or will. If that objection

be valid, He becomes to us simply an unknown cause, what men of science call force; that to which all phenomena are to be referred, but of which we know nothing. We must adhere to the truth in its Scriptural form, or we lose it altogether. We must believe that God is love in the sense in which that word comes home to every human heart. The Scriptures do not mock us when they say, 'Like as a father pitieth his children, so the Lord pitieth them that fear Him' (Ps. 103:13).[4]

We may perhaps quibble with the odd phrasing of Hodge's words, but his point is well taken. We shall consider the bearing of all this on the doctrine of impassibility in the next chapter. My chief point here is that we cannot begin to fathom the nature of the love of God by something as superficial as methodologically flawed word studies.

How to proceed: text in context

What we must do is study passages with great respect for their contexts, and themes in the Bible with great attention devoted to their place in the unfolding drama of redemption. The trouble in this case, of course, is that there are so many of both kinds, (passages and themes) that bear on the love of God that a brief treatment can barely scratch the surface. But a scratched surface is at least a start, so I shall make one scratch and probe one passage that gives us a glimpse into the intra-Trinitarian love of God and provide some rudimentary reflections on the contribution of this passage to the central theme of this book.

The passage I have in mind is John 5:16–30. Following the flow of thought uncovers extraordinary insight on the relation between the Father and the Son. It is one of two passages in this Gospel where the apostle declares that the Father loves the Son.

Jesus has just healed the paralytic at the pool. He then instructs the man to pick up his mat and walk (5:8). The healed man does so and runs afoul of the authorities who charge him with breaching the Sabbath regulations. Trying to provide clarity to the Mosaic prohibition of work on the Sabbath, Jewish scholars had developed various *halakhoth* (rules of conduct), including the prohibition against carrying any burden outside your domicile and carrying any burden higher than your shoulder, even in your domicile. Such rules became what it means not to work on the Sabbath. When the man diverts attention away from himself by blaming Jesus (5:11), official disapproval turns against Jesus because he 'was doing these things on the Sabbath' (5:16). Whether 'these things' refers specifically to the healing or to the advice that had encouraged another man to engage in a prohibited category of work, or more likely both, matters little.

Jesus might have replied by engaging in a theological dispute over the *halakhoth*. He might have pointed out that the Mosaic law was not so specific, that he himself was scarcely a medical doctor trying to earn a little extra by working overtime on the Sabbath by performing medical procedures that could have waited until the next day, and that the healed man was not a worker picking up extra pocket-money by carrying a mat on the Sabbath. Any such rejoinder would have met with heavy-duty debate but not with a charge of blasphemy. Instead, Jesus here avoids all such arguments and authorizes his own Sabbath activity by saying, 'My Father is always at his work to this very day, and I, too, am working' (5:17).

Two background features must be understood in order to grasp the implications of this claim.

(1) 'Sonship' is very often a functional category in the Bible. Because the overwhelming majority of sons ended up vocationally doing what their fathers did, 'like father, like son' was the cultural assumption. Jesus assumes as much in the Beatitudes: 'Blessed are the peacemakers, for they will be called *sons of God*' (Matt. 5:9). The idea is that God is the supreme Peacemaker, and so every peacemaker is in that respect like God, and to that extent God's 'son'. That is also the thinking that stands behind such monikers as 'son of Belial [worthlessness]' and 'son of encouragement'. The unarticulated cultural assumption is that the man in question is either so worthless or so encouraging that his father must have been, respectively, worthlessness or encouragement. So when Jesus claims that his 'Father' is 'always at his work to this very day', he is implicitly claiming to be God's Son, with the right to follow the pattern of

work that God himself sets in this regard.

(2) First-century Jewish authorities entered into sustained theological disputes over whether God kept the Sabbath. One side said he did; the other denied it, arguing that if God ceased from all his works on the Sabbath, his works of providence would stop, and the universe would collapse. But the first side seems to have been dominant. They argued in return that since the entire universe is God's domicile, and since he is so much bigger than anything in the universe that it can never be said of him that he raises anything above his own shoulders, therefore he never performs any work on the Sabbath that breaches *halakhoth*, and so he keeps the Sabbath. This means, of course, that God 'works' even on the Sabbath (and so his providential order is maintained), but that he does not 'work' in such a way as to break the Sabbath. In the nature of the case, of course, this sort of loophole could apply only to God.

Yet here is Jesus, claiming the right to work on the Sabbath *because God is his Father*, and, implicitly, he is the Son who follows in his Father's footsteps in this regard. The point is that while one may be called a son of God for being a peacekeeper, ordinary mortals cannot rightly be called sons of God *in every respect*, since they do not imitate God in every respect. I have not created a universe recently; certainly I am not a son of God with respect to *creatio ex nihilo*. The Jews recognized that the loophole that applied to God's working on the Sabbath was tied to the transcendence of God and suited him alone. For Jesus to justify his own Sabbath working by appealing to God as his Father was to make a stupendous claim. Now he was not only breaking the Sabbath, the Jews reasoned, 'but he was even calling God his own Father, making himself equal with God' (5:18).

They were right, of course, but also slightly mistaken. Almost certainly they thought of Jesus setting himself up in parallel with God, another God-centre. Implicitly the charge was blasphemy, and the construction was ditheism. In his reply in the following verses, Jesus provides the raw materials that preserve his equality with God while never sanctioning ditheism. In short, he provides the raw stuff of *Christian* monotheism. Along the way, he says some extraordinarily important things about the love of God. We cannot here take the time to follow his argument in great detail, but we may skip through the text and trace the following points.

(1) Jesus denies that he is setting himself over against God as an alternative to God. Far from it: he is entirely dependent on the Father and subordinate to him – yet it turns out to be an astonishing subordination. On the one hand: 'I tell you the truth, the Son can do nothing by himself; he can do only what he sees his Father doing' (5:19a). Thus he never threatens the Father with competition as a divine alternative. On the other hand, he can do *only* what he sees his Father doing, 'because *whatever the Father does* the Son also does' (5:19b). Here is a claim to deity slipped through the back door. It is one thing to claim to be like God in a role as

peacemaker; it is another to claim to do *whatever* the Father does. Indeed, take seriously the connection between the two clauses, and Jesus actually grounds his functional subordination in his claim to *coextensive* action with his Father. He can do only what he sees the Father doing (subordination) *because* (*gar*) he does whatever the Father does (coextensive action). That makes his sonship unique.

(2) The next verse (5:20) tells us *why it is* that the Son does everything the Father does. Whatever the Father does, the Son also does, we are told (5:19b), *for* (*gar*, 5:20) the Father loves the Son and shows him all he does. Here the pre-industrial model of the agrarian village or the craftsman's shop is presupposed, with a father carefully showing his son all that he does so that the family tradition is preserved. Stradivarius Senior shows Stradivarius Junior all there is to know about making violins – selecting the wood, the exact proportions, the cuts, the glue, how to add precisely the right amount of arsenic to the varnish, and so forth. Stradivarius Senior does this because he loves Stradivarius Junior. So also here: Jesus is so uniquely and unqualifiedly the Son of God that the Father shows him *all* he does, *out of sheer love for him*, and the Son, however dependent on his Father, does *everything* the Father does.

(3) Within the framework of Johannine theology, there are two enormously important entailments. *First*, the Son by his obedience to his Father, doing *only* what God gives him to do and saying *only* what God gives him to say, yet doing such things in

function of his ability to do *whatever* the Father does, acts in such a way as to reveal God perfectly. In other words, if the Son acted in line with the Father sometimes and did his own thing on other occasions, we would not be able to tell which of Jesus' actions and words disclose God. But it is precisely his unqualified obedience to and his dependence upon his Father that ensure that his revelation to us is perfect. Far from threatening the Son's perfections or jeopardizing his revelation of God to us, his functional subordination ensures his perfections and establishes his revelation. *Second,* this marvellous self-disclosure of the Father in the Son turns, ultimately, not on God's love for us, but on the Father's love for his unique Son. It is *because the Father loves the Son* that this pattern of divine self-disclosure pertains.

We too quickly think of our salvation almost exclusively with respect to its bearing on us. Certainly there is endless ground for wonder in the Father's love for us, in Jesus' love for us. (We shall return to these themes in due course.) But undergirding them, more basic than they are, is the Father's love for the Son. Because of the love of the Father for the Son, the Father has determined that all should honour the Son even as they honour the Father (John 5:23). Indeed, this love of the Father for the Son is what makes sense of John 3:16. True, 'God so loved the world that he gave his one and only Son' – there the object of God's love is the world. But the standard that tells us just how great that love is has already been set. What is its measure? God so loved that world *that he gave his Son.* Paul's reasoning is similar: if God did not spare *his Son*, how shall he not also with him freely give us all things (Rom. 8:32)? The argument is cogent only because the relationship between the Father and the Son is the standard for all other love relationships.

(4) Before I press on with the flow of the argument in this passage, this is the place to reflect as well on the Son's love for his Father. This theme does not overtly surface here, but it does elsewhere in John's Gospel. Because the Son always does the things that please him, the Father has not left him alone (8:29). Indeed, the perfection of the Son's obedience (he always does what the Father has commanded him, 14:31) is grounded in his love for the Father (14:31).

(5) The evangelist has told us that the Father loves the Son, a love manifest in the Father showing the Son all he does (5:20a). Indeed, the Father will show the Son 'even greater things than these ["these" referring, presumably, to the things that Jesus has already done]. For just as the Father raises the dead and gives them life, even so the Son gives life to whom he is pleased to give it' (5:20b-21). It is the prerogative of God alone to kill and make alive. In the past God occasionally used human agents in the resuscitation of someone (e.g., Elijah). Jesus is different. Because the Father has 'shown' him this, Jesus raises the dead as he pleases, just as the Father does.

It would be theologically profitable to pursue the line of argument in the text all the way to verse 30. But although that would tell us more about the nature of the Godhead, it would not greatly develop our understanding of the love of God in the Godhead. So I must draw this discussion to a close with two observations.

Some concluding synthetic reflections

First, it has sometimes been argued that the label 'the Son' is rightly attached only to the incarnate Word, not to the Word in his pre-incarnate glory.[5] This view has sometimes sought support from this passage. There seems to be progress in time as the Father 'shows' things to 'the Son', showing him resurrection later than other things – and this surely means that all of this 'showing' to the Son is tied up with the incarnational state of the Son.

Nevertheless: (1) the same passage argues that the Son does *whatever* the Father does. If this 'whatever' is comprehensive, it must include creation, which ties this Son to the Word who is God's agent in creation (John 1:2–3). If that is the case, then in addition to the Father 'showing' the Son things in eternity past (hence the Son's agency in creation), the Father also 'showed' him things, step by step, in his incarnate state, which served as the precise trigger for what Jesus in the days of his flesh actually did, and when.

(2) The obvious reading of texts such as John 3:17 ('For God did not send his Son into the world to condemn the world, but to save the world through him') is that the person sent was the Son when the Father sent him. True, such language could plausibly be anachronistic. If I say, 'My wife was born in

England several decades ago', I do not imply that she was my wife when she was born. I have heard of robbing the cradle, but this is ridiculous. But such exceptions are normally clear from the context. In a book that has already introduced the pre-existence of the Word (1:1, 14), the natural reading of 3:17 is that 'the Son' is an alternative appellation for that Word, not that this is a tag only for his incarnational existence.

(3) Had I time, I think I could demonstrate that John 5:26 most plausibly reads as an *eternal* grant from the Father to the Son, which inherently transcends time and stretches Jesus' sonship into eternity past. When the text says that the Father has 'life in himself', the most natural understanding where the subject is God is that this refers to God's self-existence. He is not dependent on anyone or anything: he has 'life in himself'.

Then we are told that God, who has 'life in himself', 'has granted the Son to have life in himself'. This is conceptually far more difficult. If the text said that the Father, who has 'life in himself', had granted to the Son to have life, there would be no conceptual difficulty, but of course the Son would then be an entirely secondary and derivative being. What would later become the doctrine of the Trinity would be ruled out.

Alternatively, if the text said that the Father has 'life in himself', and the Son has 'life in himself', there would be no conceptual difficulty, but it would be much harder to rule out ditheism. In fact, what the text says is that the Father has 'life in himself', and he *has granted* to the Son to have 'life in himself'. The expression 'life in himself' really must mean the same thing in both parts of the verse. But how can such 'life in himself', the life of self-existence, be granted by another?

The ancient explanation still seems to me the best one: this is an eternal grant. There was therefore never a time when the Son did not have 'life in himself'. This eternal grant establishes the nature of the eternal relationship between the Father and the Son. But if this is correct, since Father and Son have always been in this relationship, the sonship of Jesus is not restricted to the days of his flesh.

(4) There are texts in which Jesus addresses God as Father (and thus implicitly thinks of himself as the Son) in terms of shared experience in eternity past (notably John 17:5: '*Father*, glorify me in your presence with the glory I had with you *before the world began*').

It follows, then, that the love of the Father for the Son, and the love of the Son for the Father, which we have been considering, cannot be restricted to the peculiar relationship that pertained from the incarnation on, but is intrinsically intra-Trinitarian.

What we have, then, is a picture of God whose love, even in eternity past, even before the creation of anything, is other-oriented. This cannot be said (for instance) of Allah. Yet because the God of the Bible is one, this plurality-in-unity does not destroy his entirely appropriate self-focus as God. As we shall see in the last chapter, because he is God, he is therefore rightly jealous. To concede that he is something other than the centre of all, and rightly to be worshipped and adored, would debase his very Godhood. He is the God who, entirely rightly, does not give his glory to another (Is. 42:8).

If this were all the Bible discloses about God, we would read in its pages of a holy God of impeccable justice. But what of love? The love of Allah is providential, which, as we saw in the first chapter, is one of the ways the Bible speaks of God. But here there is more: in eternity past, the Father loved the Son, and the Son loved the Father. There has *always* been an other-orientation to the love of God. All the manifestations of the love of God emerge out of this deeper, more fundamental reality: love is bound up in the very nature of God. God is love.

Second, mark well the *distinction* between the love of the Father for the Son and the love of the Son for the Father. The Father commands, sends, tells, commissions – and demonstrates his love for the Son by 'showing' him everything, such that the Son does whatever the Father does. The Son obeys, says only what the Father gives him to say, does only what the Father gives him to do, comes into the world as the Sent One – and demonstrates his love for the Father precisely by such obedience. Not once is there any hint that the Son commissions the Father, who obeys. Not once is there a hint that the Father submits to the Son or is dependent upon him for his own words and deeds. Historically, Christians avoiding the trap of Arianism have insisted that the Son is equal with God in substance or essence, but that there is an economic or functional subordination of the Son to the Father.[6]

What is of interest to us for our topic is the way the texts distinguish how the love of the Father for the Son is manifested, and how the love of the Son for the Father is manifested – and then how such love further functions as lines are drawn outward to elements of Christian conduct and experience. These function in various ways. There is space to reflect on only one of them.

In John 15, Jesus tells his disciples, 'As the Father has loved me, so have I loved you' (15:9). Thus we move from the intra-Trinitarian love of the Father for the Son, to the Son's love of his people in redemption. Jesus thus becomes the mediator of his Father's love. Receiving love, so has he loved. Then he adds, 'Now remain in my love. If you obey my commands, you will remain in my love, just as I have obeyed my Father's commands and remain in his love' (15:9b–10).

Reflect on the parallelism. The perfection of Jesus' obedience in the Godhead, which we have just been told is the mark of the Son's love for his Father (14:31), is precisely what it means for the eternal Son to remain in the love the Father has for him. This is a *relational* matter (i.e., the Father and the Son are related to each other in this way), but it is also a *constitutional* matter (i.e., that is the way God Almighty is constituted). This pattern of love, both relational and constitutional, in the very being of God becomes, according to Jesus, the model and incentive of our relation to Jesus. If *we* love *him*, we will obey him (14:15); here, if we obey him, we remain in his love. And thereby our relation to Jesus mirrors the relation of Jesus to his heavenly Father — which is of course a major theme in John 17.

Then the passage explicitly harks back to John 5, which we have been thinking through. Jesus says, 'You are my friends if you do what I command. I no longer call you servants, because a servant does not know his master's business. Instead, I have called you friends, *for everything that I learned from my Father I have made known to you*' (15:14–15).

Observe that Jesus makes a distinction between slaves (*douloi*; not 'servants') and friends. But the distinction initially surprises us. We are Jesus' *friends* if we do what he commands. This sounds rather like a definition of a slave. Certainly such friendship is not reciprocal. I cannot turn around to Jesus and thank him for his friendship and tell him he is my friend, too, if he does everything I command him. Strange to tell, not once is Jesus or God ever described in the Bible as our friend. Abraham is God's friend; the reverse is never stated.

Of course, in one sense Jesus is the best friend a poor sinner ever had. Nevertheless, that is not the terminology of Scripture, almost as if the Bible is reluctant to descend into the kind of cheap intimacy that brings God or Jesus down to our level. In this context, what then is the difference that Jesus is drawing between slave and friend? *Our* culture teaches that the slave obeys, and the friend may or may not; clearly, however, that is not the distinction Jesus has in mind.

He says we are his friends because he has made

known to us all that he learned from his Father. An army colonel tells a GI to fetch the jeep. If the GI says he will do so only if the colonel tells him exactly why and gives him permission to use it as a runabout while the colonel spends his time at HQ, that GI is asking for about six months of kitchen patrol duty. But suppose the colonel has been a friend of the GI's family for years and has watched the young man grow up. He may say to the GI, 'Jim, fetch the jeep, please. I need you to drive me to HQ. I'll be there about two hours. You can use the vehicle in that gap, provided you're back to pick me up at 1600 hours.' In this case, of course, the GI is no less required to obey the colonel. The difference, the difference of friendship, is that full information has been conveyed. It is an informational difference, a difference of revelation, not a difference of obedience.

God's people are no longer slaves. At this point in redemptive history, the fullness of God's revelation has come to us in the Son who was perfectly obedient and thereby perfectly disclosed God. We are *no longer* slaves (a redemptive-historical marker), but friends. And what has brought this change about is that in the fullness of time God *sent* his Son into the world, and the Son *obeyed*; that the Father *in love* for the Son determined that all should honour the Son even as they honour the Father; and Father and Son, in perfect harmony of plan and vision, at the time God ordained, played out their roles – the Father sending, commissioning, 'showing', and the Son coming, revealing, disclosing what had been 'shown' him, and in obedience going to the cross.

And we, the heirs of the new covenant, are unfathomably privileged to be let in on this stupendous plan. We are the friends of God.

We are the friends of God by virtue of the intra-Trinitarian love of God that so worked out in the fullness of time that the plan of redemption, conceived in the mind of God in eternity past, has exploded into our space-time history at exactly the right moment. When the time had fully come, as Paul puts it, God sent his Son (Gal. 4:4). And we have been incalculably privileged not only to be saved by God's love, but to be shown it, to be informed about it, to be let in on the mind of God. God is love; and we are the friends of God.

3
God's love and God's sovereignty

Let me sum up. In the first chapter I outlined some factors that make the doctrine of the love of God a difficult thing to talk about. Some of these are cultural; others are bound up with the challenge of trying to integrate the many varied and complementary things the Bible says about the love of God. Further, what does such love look like in a God who is omnipotent, omniscient, sovereign, and transcendent (i.e., above space and time)? Then I briefly outlined five different ways the Bible speaks of the love of God – his intra-Trinitarian love, his providential love, his yearning and salvific love that pleads with sinners, his elective love, and his conditional love – and indicated what could go wrong if any one of them is absolutized.

In the second chapter we reflected a little on a few

texts that disclose the intra-Trinitarian love of God, and we thought through a few of the implications.

Here the focus will be on God's love for human beings, but especially in relation to his own transcendence and sovereignty. To organize the material, I shall try to establish three points.

The affective element in God's love

We have already reflected a little on attempts to strip God's love of affective content and make it no more than willed commitment to the other's good. The philology does not support this view; nor does 1 Corinthians 13, where the apostle insists it is possible to deploy the most stupendous altruism without love. But it is worth pausing to hear some specific texts where the vibrant, affective element in the love of God is almost overpowering.

One of the most striking passages is Hosea 11. Of course, the entire prophecy of Hosea is an astonishing portrayal of the love of God. Almighty God is likened to a betrayed and cuckolded husband. But the intensity of God's passion for the covenant nation comes to a climax in Hosea 11. 'When Israel was a child,' God declares, 'I loved him, and out of Egypt I called my son' (11:1). The exodus thus marks the origin of this covenant relationship.

But the more God called Israel, the more they drifted away. God was the one who cared for them, taught them to walk, and healed them. He was the one who 'led them with cords of human kindness' (11:4). Yet they did not recognize him. They sacrificed to the Baals and loved idolatry. So God promises judgment. They will return to 'Egypt' and Assyria, i.e., to captivity and slavery, 'because they refuse to repent' (11:5). Their cities will be destroyed (11:6). 'My people are determined to turn from me. Even if they call to the Most High, he will by no means exalt them' (11:7). Thus it sounds as if implacable judgment has been pronounced.

But then it is almost as if God cannot endure the thought. In an agony of emotional intensity, God cries,

> 'How can I give you up, Ephraim?
>   How can I hand you over, Israel? ...
>   How can I make you like Zeboiim?
> My heart is changed within me;
>   all my compassion is aroused.
> I will not carry out my fierce anger,
>   nor will I turn and devastate Ephraim.
> For I am God, and not man –
>   the Holy One among you.
>   I will not come in wrath.
> They will follow the LORD;
>   he will roar like a lion.
> When he roars,
>   his children will come trembling from
>   the west.
> They will come trembling
>   like birds from Egypt,
>   like doves from Assyria.
> I will settle them in their homes,'
>   declares the LORD.

The passage as a whole means that the promised impending judgment will not be the last word. Exile will be followed by return from exile. In the entire context, when God declares that his heart is changed within him and all his compassion is aroused, he does not mean that he has changed his mind and Israel will be spared the punishment he decreed a few verses earlier. Rather, it is that any long-term threat of permanent judgment must be set aside. God will bring them back from Egypt and Assyria.

At one level, this is common fare among the pre-exilic prophets. It is the emotional intensity of this passage that draws one's attention. Yet we should not be surprised. God repeatedly discloses himself to be a jealous God (as in the Decalogue), the God who abounds in 'love and faithfulness' – that glorious pair of words constantly repeated in the Old Testament and intoned to Moses as he hid in a cleft of the rock until he was permitted to peek out and glimpse something of the afterglow of the glory of God (Exod. 34:6). God grieves (Ps. 78:40; Eph. 4:30); he rejoices (Is. 62:5); his wrath burns hot against his foes (Exod. 32:10); he pities (Ps. 103:13). And as we have seen, he loves – indeed, with an everlasting love (Is. 54:8; Ps. 103:17).

We may look at the love of God from still another perspective. In passages such as 1 John 4:7–11, believers are urged to love one another since love is of God; indeed, God is love. The high point in the demonstration of God's love is his sending of his Son as the 'atoning sacrifice' for our sins. 'Dear friends,'

John concludes, 'since God so loved us, we also ought to love one another' (4:11). Do you see the point? Whatever the distinctive elements in the love of God, the same word is used for God's love and the Christian's love, and God's love is both the model and the incentive of our love. Doubtless God's love is immeasurably richer than ours, in ways still to be explored, but they belong to the same genus, or the parallelisms could not be drawn.

Many Christian traditions affirm the impassibility of God. The Westminster Confession of Faith asserts that God is 'without ... passions'. If this is taken to mean that God is emotionless, it is profoundly unbiblical and should be repudiated. But the most learned discussion over impassibility is never so simplistic. Although Aristotle may exercise more than a little scarcely recognized influence upon those who uphold impassibility, at its best impassibility is trying to avoid a picture of a God who is changeable, given over to mood swings, dependent upon his creatures. *Our* passions shape our direction and frequently control our will. What shall we say of God?

That brings us to the second point.

The sovereignty and transcendence of God

Here it will be helpful to organize what I wish to say into five parts. Initially you will have to take my word for it that this is not an excursus but highly relevant to our reflections on the love of God. Much of what I say in the next few paragraphs is no more than a spotty review. But it is essential to what will follow.

(1) God is utterly sovereign (he is both omnipotent and omniscient), and he is transcendent (in himself he exists above time and space, i.e., above the created order with its intrinsic limitations). God is omnipotent; i.e., he is able to do anything he wishes to do. Nothing is too hard for him (Jer. 32:17); he is the Almighty (2 Cor. 6:18; Rev. 1:8). Jesus insists that with God all things are possible (Matt. 19:26). His sovereignty extends over the mighty movements of the stars in their courses, over the fall of a sparrow, over the exact count of the hairs of my head. If you throw a pair of dice, what numbers come up lies in the determination of God (Prov. 16:33). Ecclesiastes shows that the ancients knew of the water cycle, but still the biblical writers preferred to say that God sends the rain. He is not the distant God espoused by deism. Through the exalted Son he upholds all things by his powerful word (Heb. 1:3); indeed, he 'works out everything in conformity with the purpose of his will' (Eph. 1:11). This control extends as much to sentient beings as to inanimate objects. He can turn the heart of the king in any direction he sees fit (Prov. 21:1). He is the potter who has the right to make out of the same lump of clay some pottery for noble purposes and some for common use (Rom. 9:21). There can be no degrees of difficulty with an omnipotent God.

Moreover, he enjoys all knowledge. He not only knows everything – he even knows what might have been under different circumstances (more or less what philosophers call 'middle knowledge'), and takes that into account when he judges (Matt. 11:20–24). There are plenty of examples where God knows what we now label free contingent future decisions (e.g., 1 Sam. 23:11–13). God's knowledge is perfect (Job 37:16). 'He does not have to reason to conclusions or ponder carefully before he answers, for he knows the end from the beginning, and he never learns and never forgets anything (cf. Ps. 90:4; 2 Peter 3:8).'[1] Precisely because he is the Creator of the universe, he must be independent from it. Indeed, in fine expressions that stretch our imagination, Isaiah affirms that God, the high and lofty one, 'lives for ever' (Is. 57:15) or 'inhabits eternity' (RSV).

(2) God's sovereignty extends to election. Election may refer to God's choice of the nation of Israel, or to God's choice of all the people of God, or to God's choice of individuals. God's choice of individuals may be for salvation or for some particular mission. Election is so important to God that he actually arranged to choose the younger of the two sons, Jacob and Esau, before they were born and therefore before either had done anything good or bad, 'in order that God's purpose in election might stand' (Rom. 9:11). Even the highly diverse ways in which new converts are described in the book of Acts reflects the comfortable, unembarrassed way New Testament writers refer to election.

We often speak of people who 'accept Jesus as their personal Saviour' – words not found in Scripture, though not necessarily wrong as a synthetic expression. But Acts may sum up some strategic evangelism by reporting that 'all who were appointed for eternal life believed' (Acts 13:48). Writing of Christians, Paul says that God 'chose us in him [i.e., Christ] before the creation of the world ... he predestined us to be adopted as his sons through Jesus Christ' (Eph. 1:4–5; cf. Rev. 13:7–8; 17:8). Indeed, God chose the Thessalonian converts from the beginning to be saved (2 Thess. 2:13).

God's election even extends to angels (1 Tim. 5:21) – which shows that election need not be tied to salvation (since there has arisen a Redeemer for fallen human beings but not for fallen angels), but is properly a function of God's sweeping sovereignty. We are a chosen race (1 Pet. 2:9).

Moreover, the Lord's electing love is immutable. All that the Father has given to the Son will come to him, and the Son will lose none of them, we are told, because he came down from heaven to do the Father's will – and this is the Father's will, that he should lose none of those the Father has given him (John 6:37–40). In other words, for the Son to lose any of those the Father has given him, he would have to be either unable or unwilling to obey his Father's explicit command. Small wonder, then, that we read that Jesus knows his own sheep, and no-one shall pluck them out of his hand.

(3) Christians are not fatalists. The central line of Christian tradition neither sacrifices the utter sovereignty of God nor reduces the responsibility of his image-bearers. In the realm of philosophical theology, this position is sometimes called compatibilism.

It simply means that God's unconditioned sovereignty and the responsibility of human beings are mutually compatible. It does not claim to show you *how* they are compatible. It claims only that we can get far enough in the evidence and the arguments to show how they are not necessarily *in*compatible, and that it is therefore entirely reasonable to think they are compatible if there is good evidence for them.[2]

The biblical evidence is compelling. When Joseph tells his fearful brothers that when they sold him into slavery, God intended it for good while they intended it for evil (Gen. 50:19–20), he is assuming compatibilism. He does not picture the event as wicked human machination into which God intervened to bring forth good. Nor does he imagine that God's intention had been to send him down there with a fine escort and a modern chariot but that unfortunately the brothers had mucked up the plan, and so poor old Joseph had to go down there as a slave – sorry about that. Rather, in one and the same event, God was operating, and his intentions were good, and the brothers were operating, and their intentions were evil.

When God addresses Assyria in Isaiah 10:5ff., he tells them that they are nothing more than tools in his hand to punish the wicked nation of Israel. However, that is not the way they see it. Because they think they are doing all this by their own strength and power, the Lord will turn around and tear them to pieces to punish their hubris after he has finished using them as a tool. That is compatibilism. There are dozens and dozens of such passages in Scripture, scattered through both Testaments.

Perhaps the most striking instance of compatibilism occurs in Acts 4:23–29. The church has suffered its first whiff of persecution. Peter and John report what has happened. The church prays to God in the language of Psalm 2. Their prayer continues (4:27–28): 'Indeed Herod and Pontius Pilate met together with the Gentiles and the people of Israel in this city to conspire against your holy servant Jesus, whom you anointed. They did what your power and will had decided beforehand should happen.' Note carefully: on the one hand, there was a terrible conspiracy that swept along Herod, Pilate, Gentile authorities, and Jewish leaders. It was a conspiracy, and they should be held accountable. On the other hand, they did what God's power and will had decided beforehand should happen.

A moment's reflection discloses that any other account of what happened would destroy biblical Christianity. If we picture the crucifixion of Jesus Christ solely in terms of the conspiracy of the local political authorities at the time, and *not* in terms of God's plan (save perhaps that he came in at the last moment and decided to use the death in a way he himself had not foreseen), then the entailment is that the cross was an accident of history. Perhaps it was an accident cleverly manipulated by God in his own interests, but it was not part of the divine plan. In that case, the entire pattern of antecedent predictive revelation is destroyed: *Yom Kippur*, the Passover lamb, the sacrificial system, and so forth. Rip Hebrews out of your Bible, for a start.[3]

On the other hand, if someone were to stress God's sovereignty in Jesus' death, exulting that all the participants 'did what [God's] power and will had decided beforehand should happen' (4:28), while forgetting that it was a wicked conspiracy, then Herod and Pilate and Judas Iscariot and the rest are exonerated of evil. If God's sovereignty means that all under it are immune from charges of transgression, then all are immune. In that case there is no sin for which atonement is necessary. So why the cross? Either way, the cross is destroyed.

In short, compatibilism is a *necessary* component to any mature and orthodox view of God and the world. Inevitably it raises important and difficult questions regarding secondary causality, how human accountability should be grounded, and much more. I cannot probe those matters here.

(4) We must briefly pause to reflect on God's immutability, his unchangeableness. 'But you remain the same, and your years will never end,' writes the psalmist (Ps. 102:27). 'I the LORD do not change' (Mal. 3:6), the Almighty declares. The entailment is that his purposes are secure and their accomplishment inevitable. 'Remember this, fix it in mind, take it to heart, you rebels. Remember the former things, those of long ago; I am God, and there is no other; I am God, and there is none like me. I make known the end from the beginning, from ancient times, what is still to come. I say: My purpose will stand, and I will do all that I please ... What I have

said, that will I bring about; what I have planned, that will I do' (Is. 46:8–11). 'But the plans of the LORD stand firm for ever, the purposes of his heart through all generations' (Ps. 33:11; cf. Matt. 13:35; 25:34; Eph. 1:4, 11; 1 Pet. 1:20).

Rightly conceived, God's immutability is enormously important. It engenders stability and elicits worship. Bavinck writes:

> The doctrine of God's immutability is of the highest significance for religion. The contrast between being and becoming marks the difference between the Creator and the creature. Every creature is continually becoming. It is changeable, constantly striving, seeks rest and satisfaction, and finds rest in God, in him alone, for only he is pure being and no becoming. Hence, in Scripture God is often called the Rock ...[4]

Yet when God's immutability is carefully discussed, theologians acknowledge that he is not immutable in every possible way or domain. He is unchanging in his being, purposes, and perfections. But this does not mean he cannot interact with his image-bearers *in their time*. The purposes of God from eternity past were to send the Son, but at a set moment in our time-space continuum the Son was actually incarnated. Even the most superficial reading of Scripture discloses God to be a personal Being who interacts with us. None of this is meant to be ruled out by immutability.

(5) Before I press on, I must frankly acknowledge that this sketch of God is coming under increasing attack, not only from numerous process theologians whose primary recourse is to philosophical analysis and synthesis, but also from some who seek to ground their work in the Bible. This view is now sometimes called the 'open' view of God.[5] Sophisticated responses are now beginning to appear, though I cannot track the debate here. But some of these writers appeal to the approximately thirty-five texts where God is clearly said to 'repent' (AV) or 'relent' (NIV) or change his mind. What shall we make of these texts?

God relents over a step he has already taken (Gen. 6:6–7; 1 Sam. 15:11, 35). He relents over what he has said he would do or even started doing (Pss. 90:13; 106:44–45; Jer. 18:7–10; 26:3, 13, 19; Joel 2:13–14; Jonah 3:9–10; 4:2), sometimes in response to the prayer of an intercessor (Exod. 32:12–14; Amos 7:3–6). For those in the 'openness of God' camp, these sorts of texts control the discussion, and the passages already discussed that affirm God's immutability are the ones that must be softened or explained away.

I do not see how this can be responsibly done.[6] Many of these texts relate to God's refusing to destroy some party because that party has repented (e.g., God relenting in the matter of destroying Nineveh because the city repents, Jonah 3:9–10). Mind you, some of the prophets *tell* their readers that that is what God's purpose has been all along when he makes such threats (e.g., Ezek. 3:16–21;

33). This is simply a way of saying that God's purposes are immutable when the situation is such and such; his purposes are different for a different set of circumstances. As for God relenting in response to the prayers of his people, one cannot think of such prayer warriors arising apart from God raising them up, whether Moses or Amos; yet on the other hand, he condemns the people for *not* producing intercessors in the hour of need (e.g., Ezek. 22:30–31). This is compatibilism: the same components recur. God remains sovereign over everything, and his purposes are good; he interacts with human beings; human beings sometimes do things well, impelled by God's grace, and he gets the credit; we frequently do things that are wicked, and although we never escape the outermost bounds of God's sovereignty, we alone are responsible and must take the blame.

I do not claim that any of this is easy or straightforward. Sooner or later one retreats into the recognition that, so far as we are concerned, there are some mysteries in the very Being of God. The deepest of these, I think, are tied to the fact that God as he has disclosed himself in Scripture is simultaneously sovereign/transcendent and personal.

Let me unpack each of these two poles. *First*, with respect to God's sovereignty and transcendence, clearly we cannot experience at some personal level what it means to be utterly sovereign or genuinely transcendent. We are finite creatures tied to time and space, with impregnable limitations on our authority and power. But we can do two things. (a) We can extrapolate what authority and power mean until we glimpse in imagination what absolute sovereignty means, and we see that that is what Scripture ascribes to God. (b) Sometimes we can proceed by reflective negations. As little as we know about time and space, we can roughly imagine what transcendence means by such a series of negations (transcendence is *not* being tied to time; it is *not* being tied to space), and we see that the Bible can talk about God that way.

Second, by way of contrast, 'personal' in our experience is so tied to finite beings interacting with finite beings that it is difficult for us to attach 'personal' to God. If I enter into a 'personal' friendship with you, I ask questions, get to know you, share things with you, find myself rebuked by you, rebuke you in return, surprise you, listen to your conversation, learn what I did not know, and so on. Sequence and finitude are presupposed. And you experience the same things at the other end of this 'personal' relationship.

But what does it mean to have a personal relationship with the transcendent, sovereign God? We cannot easily imagine this, *whether by extrapolation of our finite experience or by strategic negations.* We can see from his gracious revelation in Scripture and in Jesus himself that this God is personal, but it is difficult for us to conceive exactly what that means. Lose that element, and you retreat into deism or pantheism or worse. We must maintain an active insistence on his personhood, but if we remain faithful to Scripture, we end up acknowledging some profound mysteries.

God's sovereign transcendence and his person-hood are both maintained in the Bible. They are both parts of the *givens*. Elevate his personhood to the exclusion of his transcendent sovereignty, and sooner or later you have a finite God, progressively reduced, and certainly not the God of the Bible. You destroy one of the *givens*. That is the track being adopted by the proponents of the 'open'-God portrait. Here I can do no more than firmly set it aside in favour of biblical compatibilism and press on toward my third point.

A rightly constrained impassibility

We are now in a position to reflect on the affective element in the love of God and its relation to God in his transcendence and sovereignty. We might provocatively ask: if God is utterly sovereign, and if he is utterly all-knowing, what space is left for emotions as we think of them? The divine oracles that picture God in pain or joy or love surely seem a little out of place, do they not, when this God knows the end from the beginning, cannot be surprised, and remains in charge of the whole thing anyway?

From such a perspective, is it not obvious that the doctrine of the love of God is difficult?

It is no answer to espouse a form of impassibility that denies that God has an emotional life and that insists that all of the biblical evidence to the contrary is nothing more than anthropopathism. The price is too heavy. You may then rest in God's sovereignty, but you can no longer rejoice in his love. You may rejoice only in a linguistic expression that is an accommodation of some reality of which we cannot conceive, couched in the anthropopathism of love. Give me a break. Paul did not pray that his readers might be able to grasp the height and depth and length and breadth of an anthropopathism and know this anthropopathism that surpasses knowledge (Eph. 3:14–21).

Nor is it adequate to suggest a solution that insists that the immanent Trinity (which refers to God as he is in himself, transcendent from the creation and focusing on his internal acts) is utterly impassible, while the economic Trinity (which refers to God as he is immanent in his creation, focusing solely on God's deeds outside of himself and in relation to his creation) does indeed suffer, including the suffering of love.[7] I worry over such a great divorce between God as he is in himself and God as he interacts with the created order. Such distinctions have heuristic usefulness now and then, but the resulting synthesis in this case is so far removed from what the Bible actually says that I fear we are being led down a blind alley. If, because the Father loves the Son and the Son loves the Father, we affirm the love of God as he is in himself (the immanent Trinity), how is that love of God connected with the love of God as he interacts with the world (the economic Trinity), which is clearly a vulnerable love that feels the pain and pleads for repentance? John, after all, clearly connects the two.

Yet before we utterly write off the impassibility of God, we must gratefully recognize what that doctrine is seeking to preserve. It is trying to ward off the kind of sentimentalizing views of the love of God and of other emotions ('passions') in God that ultimately make him a souped-up human being but no more. For instance, a God who is terribly vulnerable to the pain caused by our rebellion is scarcely a God who is in control or a God who is so perfect that he does not, strictly speaking, *need* us. The modern therapeutic God may be superficially attractive because he appeals to *our* emotions, but the cost will soon be high. Implicitly we start thinking of a finite God. God himself is gradually diminished and reduced from what he actually is. And that is idolatry.

Closer to the mark is the recognition that all of God's emotions, including his love in all its aspects, cannot be divorced from God's knowledge, God's power, God's will. If God loves, it is because he chooses to love; if he suffers, it is because he chooses to suffer. God is impassible in the sense that he sustains no 'passion', no emotion, that makes him vulnerable from the outside, over which he has no control, or which he has not foreseen.

Equally, however, all of God's will or choice or plan is never divorced from his love – just as it is never divorced from his justice, his holiness, his omniscience, and all his other perfections. Thus I am not surreptitiously retreating to a notion of love that is merely willed altruism; I am not suggesting that God's love be dissolved in God's will. Rather, I am suggesting that we will successfully guard against the evils that impassibility combats if we recognize that

God's 'passions', unlike ours, do not flare up out of control. *Our* passions change our direction and priorities, domesticating our will, controlling our misery and our happiness, surprising and destroying or establishing our commitments. But *God's* 'passions', like everything else in God, are displayed in conjunction with the fullness of all his other perfections. In that framework, God's love is not so much a function of his will, as something that displays itself in perfect harmony with his will – and with his holiness, his purposes in redemption, his infinitely wise plans, and so forth.

Of course, this means that in certain respects God's love does not function exactly like ours. How could it? God's love emanates from an infinite Being whose perfections are immutable. But this way of wording things guards the most important values in impassibility and still insists that God's love is real love, of the same genus as the best of love displayed by God's image-bearers. And if large areas of uncertainty remain as to how all this works out in the being and action of God, I suspect it is because we have returned by another route to the abiding tension between the biblical portrait of the sovereign, transcendent God and the biblical portrait of the personal God – and thus to the very mystery of God.

This approach to these matters accounts well for certain biblical truths of immense practical importance. God does not 'fall in love' with the elect; he does not 'fall in love' with us; he *sets his affection* on us. He does not predestine us out of some stern whimsy; rather, *in love* he predestines us to be adopted as his sons (Eph. 1:4–5).[8] *The texts themselves tie the love of God to other perfections in God.*

We may gain clarity by an example. Picture Charles and Susan walking down a beach hand in hand at the end of the academic year. The pressure of the term has dissipated in the warm evening breeze. They have kicked off their sandals, and the wet sand squishes between their toes. Charles turns to Susan, gazes deeply into her large, hazel eyes, and says, 'Susan, I love you. I really do.'

What does he mean?

Well, in this day and age he may mean nothing more than that he feels like testosterone on legs and wants to go to bed with her forthwith. But if we assume he has even a modicum of decency, let alone Christian virtue, the least he means is something like this: 'Susan, you mean everything to me. I can't live without you. Your smile knocks me out from fifty metres. Your sparkling good humour, your beautiful eyes, the scent of your hair – everything about you transfixes me. I love you!'

What he most certainly does *not* mean is something like this: 'Susan, quite frankly you have such a bad case of halitosis it would embarrass a herd of unwashed, garlic-eating elephants. Your nose is so bulbous you belong in the cartoons. Your hair is so greasy it could lubricate an eighteen-wheeler. Your knees are so disjointed you make a camel look elegant. Your personality makes Attila the Hun and Genghis Khan look like wimps. But I love you!'

So now God comes to us and says, 'I love you.' What does he mean?

Does he mean something like this? 'You mean everything to me. I can't live without you. Your personality, your witty conversation, your beauty, your smile – everything about you transfixes me. Heaven would be boring without you. I love you!' That, after all, is pretty close to what some therapeutic approaches to the love of God spell out. We must be pretty wonderful because God loves us. And dear old God is pretty vulnerable, finding himself in a dreadful state unless we say yes. Suddenly serious Christians unite and rightly cry, 'Bring back impassibility!'

When he says he loves us, does not God rather mean something like the following? 'Morally speaking, you are the people of the halitosis, the bulbous nose, the greasy hair, the disjointed knees, the abominable personality. Your sins have made you disgustingly ugly. But I love you anyway, not because you are attractive, but because it is my nature to love.' And in the case of the elect, God adds, 'I have set my affection on you from before the foundation of the universe, not because you are wiser or better or stronger than others but because in grace I chose to love you. You are mine, and you will be transformed. Nothing in all creation can separate you from my love mediated through Jesus Christ' (Rom. 8).

Isn't that a little closer to the love of God depicted in Scripture? Doubtless the Father finds the Son lovable; doubtless in the realm of disciplining his covenant people, there is a sense in which his love is conditioned by our moral conformity. But at the end of the day, God loves, whomever the object, because

God is love. There are thus two critical points. *First*, God exercises this love in conjunction with all his other perfections, but his love is no less love for all that. *Second*, his love emanates from his own character; it is not dependent on the loveliness of the loved, external to himself.

John's point in 1 John 4, 'God is love', is that those who really do know God come to love that way too. Doubtless we do not do it very well, but aren't Christians supposed to love the unlovable – even our enemies? Because we have been transformed by the gospel, our love is to be self-originating, not elicited by the loveliness of the loved. For that is the way it is with God. He loves because love is one of his perfections, in perfect harmony with all his other perfections.

At our best, we know that that is the way God's image-bearers should love too. In one of her loveliest sonnets, never written to be published, Elizabeth Barrett Browning wrote to her husband Robert Browning:

If thou must love me, let it be for naught,
Except for love's sake only. Do not say,
'I love her for her smile – her looks – her way
Of speaking gently – for a trick of thought
That falls in well with me, and certes brought
A sense of pleasant ease on such a day.'
For these things, in themselves, Beloved, may
Be changed, or change for thee – and love,
   so wrought,
May be unwrought so. Neither love me for

Thine own dear pity's wiping my cheeks dry –
A creature might forget to weep, who bore
Thy comfort long, and lose thy love thereby!
But love me for love's sake, that evermore
Thou may'st love on, through love's eternity.

And this, brothers and sisters, we have learned
from God as he has disclosed himself in his Son; for
'we love because he first loved us' (1 John 4:19).
'While we were still sinners, Christ died for us'
(Rom. 5:8). Here is love, not that we loved God, but
that he loved us, and gave his Son to be the
propitiation for our sins (1 John 4:10).

4

God's love and God's wrath

Many think it is easy for God to forgive. I recall
meeting a young and articulate French West African
when I was studying in Germany more than twenty
years ago. We were both working diligently to
improve our German, but once a week or so we had
had enough, so we went out for a meal together and
retreated to French, a language we both knew well.
In the course of those meals we got to know each
other. I learned that his wife was in London training
to be a medical doctor. He himself was an engineer
who needed fluency in German in order to pursue
doctoral studies in engineering in Germany.

Pretty soon I discovered that once or twice a week
he disappeared into the red light district of town.
Obviously he went to pay his money and have his
woman. Eventually I got to know him well enough

to ask him what he would do if he discovered that his wife were doing something similar in London.

'Oh,' he said, 'I'd kill her.'

'That's a bit of a double standard, isn't it?' I replied.

'You don't understand. Where I come from in Africa, the husband has the right to sleep with many women, but if a wife does it, she must be killed.'

'But you told me that you were raised in a mission school. You know that the God of the Bible does not have double standards like that.'

He gave me a bright smile and replied, 'Ah, *le bon Dieu; il doit nous pardonner; c'est son métier* [Ah, God is good; he's bound to forgive us; that's his job].'

It is a common view, is it not? I do not know if my African friend knew that the same words are ascribed to Catherine the Great; he may have been consciously quoting her, for he was well read. But even when people do not put things quite so bluntly, the idea is popular, not least because, as we have seen, some ill-defined notions of the love of God run abroad in the land – but these notions have been sadly sentimentalized and horribly stripped of all the complementary things the Bible has to say.

In this last chapter I want to reflect on just a few of these other things, with the aim of thinking more precisely and faithfully about the love of God.

The love of God and the wrath of God

Here I shall venture three reflections.

(1) The Bible speaks of the wrath of God in high-

intensity language. 'The LORD Almighty is mustering an army for war ... Wail, for the day of the LORD is near; it will come like destruction from the Almighty ... See, the day of the LORD is coming – a cruel day, with wrath and fierce anger – to make the land desolate and destroy the sinners within it' (Is. 13:4, 6, 9). 'Therefore as surely as I live, declares the Sovereign LORD, because you have defiled my sanctuary with all your vile images and detestable practices, I myself will withdraw my favour; I will not look on you with pity or spare you. A third of your people will die of the plague or perish by famine inside you; a third will fall by the sword outside your walls; and a third I will scatter to the winds and pursue with drawn sword ... And when I have spent my wrath upon them, they will know that I the LORD have spoken in my zeal. I will make you a ruin and a reproach among the nations around you, in the sight of all who pass by ... When I shoot at you with my deadly and destructive arrows of famine, I will shoot to destroy you ... Plague and bloodshed will sweep through you, and I will bring the sword against you. I the LORD have spoken' (Ezek. 5:11–17). Such passages could be multiplied a hundredfold. Make all the allowance you like for the nature of language in the apocalyptic genre, but Revelation 14 includes some of the most violent expressions of God's wrath found in all literature.

Wrath, like love, includes emotion as a necessary component. Here again, if impassibility is defined in terms of the complete absence of all 'passions', not only will you fly in the face of the biblical evidence, but you tumble into fresh errors that touch the very holiness of God. The reason is that in itself, wrath, unlike love, is *not* one of the intrinsic perfections of God. Rather, it is a function of God's holiness against sin. Where there is no sin, there is no wrath – but there will always be love in God. Where God in his holiness confronts his image-bearers in their rebellion, there *must* be wrath, or God is not the jealous God he claims to be, and his holiness is impugned. The price of diluting God's wrath is diminishing God's holiness.

This point is so important I must tease it out a little further. It is hard to read the pages of Scripture without perceiving that the wrath of God, however much it is a function of God's holiness against sin, nevertheless has a powerful affective element in it. Thus to distance God too greatly from wrath on the ground of a misconceived form of impassibility soon casts shadows back on to his holiness.

Alternatively, this so-called wrath, depersonalized and de-emotionalized, is redefined as an anthropo-pathism that is actually talking about the impartial and inevitable *impersonal* effects of sin in a person or culture. That was the route of C. H. Dodd in the 1930s. The entailment, then as now, is that the significance of the cross changes. If God is not really angry, it is difficult to see why any place should be preserved for propitiation. But to this I shall return.

Further, to retreat to the distinction between the immanent Trinity and the economic Trinity in this case would be disastrous. That tactic argues that God as he is in himself (the immanent Trinity) is immune from wrath while God as he interacts with rebels (the economic Trinity) displays his wrath. But because God's wrath is a function of his holiness, this leaves us in the dubious position of ascribing to God as he is in himself less concern for maintaining his holiness than God as he interacts with the created and fallen order. Conceptually this is a substantial distance from the pictures of God in Scripture; analytically it is slightly bizarre.

(2) How, then, should the love of God and the wrath of God be understood to relate to each other? One evangelical cliché has it that God hates the sin but loves the sinner. There is a small element of truth in these words: God has nothing but hate for the sin, but it would be wrong to conclude that God has nothing but hate for the sinner. A difference must be maintained between God's view of sin and his view of the sinner. Nevertheless the cliché (God hates the sin but loves the sinner) is false on the face of it and should be abandoned. Fourteen times in the first fifty psalms alone, we are told that God hates the sinner, his wrath is on the liar, and so forth. In the Bible, the wrath of God rests both on the sin (Rom. 1:18ff.) and on the sinner (John 3:36).

Our problem, in part, is that in human experience wrath and love normally abide in mutually exclusive compartments. Love drives wrath out, or wrath drives love out. We come closest to bringing them together, perhaps, in our responses to a wayward act by one of our children, but normally we do not think that a wrathful person is loving.

But this is not the way it is with God. God's wrath

is not an implacable, blind rage. However emotional it may be, it is an entirely reasonable and willed response to offences against his holiness. But his love, as we saw in the last chapter, wells up amidst his perfections *and is not generated by the loveliness of the loved*. Thus there is nothing intrinsically impossible about wrath and love being directed toward the same individual or people at the same time. God in his perfections must be wrathful against his rebel image-bearers, for they have offended him; God in his perfections must be loving toward his rebel image-bearers, for he is that kind of God.

(3) Two other misconceptions circulate widely even in circles of confessional Christianity.

The *first* is that in the Old Testament God's wrath is more strikingly transparent than his love, while in the New Testament, though doubtless a residue of wrath remains, a gentleness takes over and softens the darker period: God's love is now richer than his wrath. After all, Jesus taught his disciples to love their enemies and turn the other cheek.

Nothing could be further from the truth than this reading of the relationship between the Testaments. One suspects that the reason why this formula has any credibility at all is that the manifestation of God's wrath in the Old Testament is primarily in *temporal* categories – famine, plague, siege, war, slaughter. In our present focus on the here and now, these images have a greater impact on us than what the New Testament says, with its focus on wrath in the afterlife. Jesus, after all, is the one who in the New Testament speaks most frequently and most colourfully about hell – this Jesus of the other cheek. The apostolic writings, climaxing in Revelation 14, offer little support for the view that a kinder, gentler God surfaces in the New Testament at this stage in redemptive history.

The reality is that the Old Testament displays the grace and love of God in experience and types, and these realities become all the clearer in the new covenant writings. Similarly, the Old Testament displays the righteous wrath of God in experience and types, and these realities become all the clearer in the new covenant writings. In other words, both God's love and God's wrath are ratcheted up in the move from the old covenant to the new, from the Old Testament to the New. These themes barrel along through redemptive history, unresolved, until they come to a resounding climax – in the cross.

Do you wish to see God's love? Look at the cross.

Do you wish to see God's wrath? Look at the cross.

Hymnwriters have sometimes captured this best. In Wales, Christians sing a nineteenth-century hymn by William Rees:

> Here is love, vast as the ocean,
>   Lovingkindness as the flood,
> When the Prince of life, our ransom,
>   Shed for us His precious blood.
> Who His love will not remember?
>   Who can cease to sing His praise?
> He can never be forgotten
>   Throughout heaven's eternal days.

> On the Mount of Crucifixion
>> Fountains opened deep and wide;
> Through the floodgates of God's mercy
>> Flowed a vast and gracious tide.
> Grace and love, like mighty rivers,
>> Poured incessant from above,
> And heaven's peace and perfect justice
>> Kissed a guilty world in love.

That brings us to the *second* common misconception. This one pictures God as implacably opposed to us and full of wrath, but somehow mollified by Jesus, who loves us. Once again, if we maintain the right frame, there is some wonderful truth here. The Epistle to the Hebrews certainly lends some support to this way of thinking, especially in its portrayal of Jesus as the high priest who continuously makes intercession to God for us. All of this is modelled on the cultus established at Sinai – or, more precisely, the cultus established at Sinai is meant to be, according to Hebrews, the shadow of the ultimate reality. Again, in 1 John 2:2 Jesus is the Advocate who speaks to the Father in our defence.

But there are other strands of New Testament theology that must be brought to bear. It was God who loved the world so much that he gave his Son (John 3:16). Here it is not that God is reluctant while his Son wins him over; rather, it is God himself who sends his Son. Thus (to return to Hebrews), even if our great high priest intercedes for us and pleads his own blood on our behalf, we must never think of this as an independent action that the Father somehow did not know about or reluctantly approved, eventually won over by the independently originating sacrifice of his Son. Rather, Father and Son are one in this project of redemption. The Son himself comes into the world by the express command of the Father.

Thus, when we use the language of propitiation, we are not to think that the Son, full of love, offered himself and thereby placated (i.e., rendered propitious) the Father, full of wrath. The picture is more complex. It is that the Father, full of righteous wrath against us, nevertheless loved us so much that he sent his Son. Perfectly mirroring his Father's words and deeds, the Son stood over against us in wrath – it is not for nothing that the Scriptures portray sinners wanting to hide from the face of him who sits on the throne *and from the wrath of the Lamb* – yet, obedient to his Father's commission, offered himself on the cross. He did this out of love both for his Father, whom he obeys, and for us, whom he redeems. Thus God is necessarily both the subject and the object of propitiation. He provides the propitiating sacrifice (he is the subject), and he himself is propitiated (he is the object). That is the glory of the cross.

All this is implicit in the great atonement passage of Romans 3:21–26. After devoting two and a half chapters to showing how the entire race is cursed and rightly under the wrath of God because of its sin (1:18 – 3:20), the apostle Paul expounds how Christ's death was *God's* wise plan 'to demonstrate his justice at the present time, so as to be just and the one who justifies those who have faith in Jesus' (Rom. 3:26). *God* presented Jesus as a propitiation in his blood, received through faith (Rom. 3:25).

The love of God and the intent of the atonement

Here I wish to see if the approaches we have been following with respect to the love of God may shed some light on another area connected with the sovereignty of God – the purpose of the atonement.

The label 'limited atonement' is singularly unfortunate for two reasons. *First*, it is a defensive, restrictive expression: here is atonement, and then someone wants to limit it. The notion of limiting something as glorious as the atonement is intrinsically offensive. *Second*, even when inspected more coolly, 'limited atonement' is objectively misleading. Every view of the atonement 'limits' it in some way, save for the view of the unqualified universalist. For example, the Arminian limits the atonement by regarding it as merely potential for everyone; the Calvinist regards the atonement as definite and effective (i.e., those for whom Christ died will certainly be saved), but limits this effectiveness to the elect; the Amyraldian limits the atonement in much the same way as the Arminian, even though the undergirding structures are different.

It may be less prejudicial, therefore, to distinguish general atonement and definite atonement, rather than unlimited atonement and limited atonement.

The Arminian (and the Amyraldian, whom I shall lump together for the sake of this discussion) holds that the atonement is general, i.e., sufficient for all, available to all, on condition of faith; the Calvinist holds that the atonement is definite, i.e., intended by God to be effective for the elect.

At least part of the argument in favour of definite atonement runs as follows. Let us grant, for the sake of argument, the truth of election.[1] That is one point where this discussion intersects with what was said in the third chapter about God's sovereignty and his electing love. In that case the question may be framed in this way: when God sent his Son to the cross, did he think of the effect of the cross with respect to his elect differently from the way in which he thought of the effect of the cross with respect to all others? If one answers negatively, it is very difficult to see that one is really holding to a doctrine of election at all; if one answers positively, then one has veered toward some notion of definite atonement. The definiteness of the atonement turns rather more on God's *intent* in Christ's cross work than in the mere *extent* of its significance.

But the issue is not merely one of logic dependent on election. Those who defend definite atonement cite texts. Jesus will save *his people* from their sins (Matt. 1:21) – not everyone. Christ gave himself 'for *us*', i.e., for us the people of the new covenant (Titus 2:14), 'to redeem *us* from all wickedness and to purify for himself *a people that are his very own*, eager to do what is good.' Moreover, in his death Christ did not merely make adequate provision for the elect, but he actually achieved the desired result (Rom. 5:6–10; Eph. 2:15–16). The Son of Man came to give his life a ransom 'for many' (Matt. 20:28; Mark 10:45; cf. Is. 53:10–12). Christ 'loved *the church* and gave himself up *for her*' (Eph. 5:25).

The Arminian, however, responds that there are simply too many texts on the other side of the issue. God so loved *the world* that he gave his Son (John 3:16). Clever exegetical devices that make 'the world' a label for referring to the elect are not very convincing. Christ Jesus is the propitiation 'for our sins, and not only for ours but also for the sins of the whole world' (1 John 2:2). And much more of the same.

So how shall we forge ahead? The arguments marshalled on both sides are of course more numerous and more sophisticated than I have indicated in this thumbnail sketch. But recall for a moment the outline I provided in the first chapter on the various ways the Bible speaks about the love of God: (1) God's intra-Trinitarian love, (2) God's love displayed in his providential care, (3) God's yearning warning and invitation to all human beings as he invites and commands them to repent and believe, (4) God's special love toward the elect, and (5) God's conditional love toward his covenant people as he speaks in the language of discipline. I indicated that if you absolutize any one of these ways in which the Bible speaks of the love of God, you will generate a false system that squeezes out other important things the Bible says, thus finally distorting your vision of God.

In this case, if we adopt the fourth of these ways of talking about God's love (viz. God's peculiar and effective love toward the elect), and insist that this is the *only* way the Bible speaks of the love of God, then definite atonement is exonerated, but at the cost of other texts that do not easily fit into this mould and at the expense of being able to say that there is any sense in which God displays a loving, yearning, salvific stance toward the whole world. Further, there could then be no sense in which the atonement is sufficient for all without exception. Alternatively, if you put all your theological eggs into the third basket and think of God's love exclusively in terms of open invitation to all human beings, one has excluded not only definite atonement as a theological construct, but also a string of passages that, read most naturally, mean that Jesus Christ did die in some special way for his own people and that God with perfect knowledge of the elect saw Christ's death with respect to the elect differently from the way in which he saw Christ's death with respect to everyone else.

Surely it is best not to introduce disjunctions where God himself has not introduced them. If one holds that the atonement is sufficient for all and effective for the elect, then both sets of texts and concerns are accommodated. As far as I can see, a text such as 1 John 2:2 states something about the potential breadth of the atonement. As I understand the historical context, the proto-gnostic opponents John was facing thought of themselves as an ontological élite who enjoyed the inside track with

God because of the special insight they had received.[2] But when Jesus Christ died, John rejoins, it was not for the sake of, say, the Jews only or, now, of some group, gnostic or otherwise, that sets itself up as intrinsically superior. Far from it. It was not for our sins only, but also for the sins of the whole world. The context, then, understands this to mean something like 'potentially for all without distinction' rather than 'effectively for all without exception' – for in the latter case all without exception must surely be saved, and John does not suppose that that will take place. This is in line, then, with passages that speak of God's love in the third sense listed above. But it is difficult to see why that should rule out the fourth sense in other passages.

In recent years I have tried to read both primary and secondary sources on the doctrine of the atonement from Calvin on.[3] One of my most forceful impressions is that the categories of the debate gradually shift with time so as to force disjunction where a slightly different bit of question-framing would allow synthesis. Correcting this, I suggest, is one of the useful things we may accomplish from an adequate study of the love of God in holy Scripture. For God is a person. Surely it is unsurprising if the love that characterizes him as a person is manifest in a variety of ways toward other persons. But it is always love, for all that.

I argue, then, that both Arminians and Calvinists should rightly affirm that Christ died for all, in the sense that Christ's death was sufficient for all and that Scripture portrays God as inviting, commanding, and desiring the salvation of all, *out of love* (in the third sense developed in the first chapter). Further, all Christians ought also to confess that, in a slightly different sense, Christ Jesus, in the intent of God, died effectively for the elect alone, *in line with the way the Bible speaks of God's special selecting love for the elect* (in the fourth sense developed in the first chapter).

Pastorally, there are many important implications. I mention only two.

(1) This approach, I contend, must surely come as a relief to young preachers in the Reformed tradition who hunger to preach the gospel effectively but who do not know how far they can go in saying things such as 'God loves you' to unbelievers. When I have preached or lectured in Reformed circles, I have often been asked the question, 'Do you feel free to tell unbelievers that God loves them?' No doubt the question is put to me because I still do a fair bit of evangelism, and people want models. Historically, Reformed theology at its best has never been slow in evangelism. Ask George Whitefield, for instance. From what I have already said, it is obvious that I have no hesitation in answering this question from young Reformed preachers affirmatively: *of course* I tell the unconverted that God loves them.

Not for a moment am I suggesting that when one preaches evangelistically, one ought to retreat to passages of the third type (above), holding back on the fourth type until after a person is converted. There is something sleazy about that sort of approach. Certainly it is possible to preach evangelistically when dealing with a passage that explicitly teaches election. Spurgeon did this sort of thing regularly. But I am saying that, provided there is an honest commitment to preaching the whole counsel of God, preachers in the Reformed tradition should not hesitate for an instant to declare the love of God for a lost world, for lost individuals. The Bible's ways of speaking about the love of God are comprehensive enough not only to permit this but to mandate it.[4]

(2) At the same time, to preserve the notion of particular redemption proves pastorally important for many reasons. If Christ died for all people with exactly the same intent, as measured on any axis, then it is surely impossible to avoid the conclusion that the *ultimate* distinguishing mark between those who are saved and those who are not is their own decision, their own will. That is surely ground for boasting. This argument does not charge the Arminian with no understanding of grace. After all, the Arminian believes that the cross is the ground of the Christian's acceptance before God; the choice to believe is not in any sense the ground. Still, this view of grace surely requires the conclusion that the *ultimate distinction between the believer and the unbeliever* lies, finally, in the human beings themselves. That entails an understanding of grace quite different, and in my view far more limited, than the view that traces the ultimate distinction back to the purposes of God, including his purposes in the cross. The pastoral implications are many and obvious.

The love of God for the world

One of the striking formal dissonances in the Johannine corpus is the superficial clash between the Gospel's assertion of the love of God for the world (John 3:16) and the first epistle's *prohibition* of love for the world (1 John 2:15–17). In brief, God loves the world, and Christians had better not. The impression is pretty strong that if people love the world, they remain under God's wrath: the love of the Father is not in them. The dissonance, of course, is merely formal. There is a ready explanation, as we shall see. But this formal dissonance reminds us yet again that the ways the Bible speaks of something are diverse and contextually controlled.

God's love for the world is commendable because it manifests itself in awesome self-sacrifice; our love for the world is repulsive when it lusts for evil participation. God's love for the world is praise-worthy because it brings the transforming gospel to it; our love for the world is ugly because we seek to be conformed to the world. God's love for the world issues in certain individuals being called out from the world and into the fellowship of Christ's followers; our love for the world is sickening where we wish to be absorbed into the world.

So 'do not love the world or anything in the world. If anyone loves the world, the love of the Father [whether this love is understood in the subjective or the objective sense] is not in him' (1 John 2:15). But clearly we are to love the world in the sense that we are to go into every part of it and bring the glorious gospel to every creature. In this sense we imitate, in our small ways, the wholly praiseworthy love of God for the world.

The love of God and the people of God

I conclude with three brief reflections.

(1) The love of God for his people is sometimes likened to the love of a parent for the child (e.g., Heb. 12:4–11; cf. Prov. 4:20). The Lord disciplines those he loves (the fifth category from the first chapter). I have said least about that category in this book. But we must never forget that we are held responsible to keep ourselves in the love of God (Jude 21), remembering that God is loving and merciful *to those who love him and who keep his commandments* (Exod. 20:6). In this, as we saw in the second chapter, we imitate Jesus. As he obeys his heavenly Father and remains in his love, so we are to obey Jesus and remain in his love (John 15:9–11).

(2) The love of God is not merely to be analysed, understood, and adopted into holistic categories of integrated theological thought. It is to be received, to be absorbed, to be felt. Meditate long and frequently on Paul's prayer in Ephesians 3:14–21. The relevant section finds the apostle praying for the believers in these terms: 'I pray that you, being rooted and established in love, may have power, together with all the saints, to grasp how wide and long and high and deep is the love of Christ, and to know this love that surpasses knowledge – that you may be filled to the measure of all the fullness of God.' Paul connects

such Christian experience of the love of God with Christian maturity, with being 'filled to the measure of all the fullness of God' (3:19), as he puts it. It is far from clear that anyone can be a mature Christian who does not walk in this path.[5]

(3) Never, never underestimate the power of the love of God to break down and transform the most amazingly hard individuals. One of the most powerful recent affirmations of this truth in a context far removed from our church buildings is the worldwide showings of the musical version of *Les Misérables*, Victor Hugo's magnificent novel. Sentenced to a nineteen-year term of hard labour for stealing bread, Jean Valjean becomes a hard and bitter man. No-one could break him; everyone feared him. Released from prison, Valjean finds it difficult to survive, as innkeepers will not welcome him and work is scarce. Then a kind bishop welcomes him into his home. But Valjean betrays the trust. During the night he creeps off into the darkness, stealing some of the family silver.

But Valjean is brought back next morning to the bishop's door by three policemen. They had arrested him and found the stolen silver on him. A word from the bishop, and the wretch would be incarcerated for life. But the bishop instantly exclaims, 'So here you are! I'm delighted to see you. Had you forgotten that I gave you the candlesticks as well? They're silver like the rest, and worth a good 200 francs. Did you forget to take them?'

Jean Valjean is released, and he is transformed. When the gendarmes withdraw, the bishop insists on giving the candlesticks to his speechless, mortified, thankful guest. 'Do not forget, do not ever forget that you have promised me to use the money to make yourself an honest man,' admonishes the bishop. And meanwhile the detective constantly pursuing Valjean, Javert, who is consumed by justice but who knows nothing of forgiveness or compassion, crumbles when his black-and-white categories of mere justice fail to cope with grace that goes against every instinct for revenge. Valjean is transformed; Javert jumps off a bridge and drowns in the Seine.

Of course, this is Christian love – i.e., the love of God mediated in this case through a bishop. But this is how it should be, for God's love so transforms us that we mediate it to others, who are thereby transformed. We love because he first loved us; we forgive because we stand forgiven.

One of the faces of love I have virtually ignored in this series of addresses is *our* love. My focus has been on the love *of God* and the various ways the Bible speaks of that love. Yet sooner or later one cannot adequately grasp the love of God in Scripture without reflecting on the ways in which God's love *elicits* our love.

To use the categories I developed in the first chapter and keep redeploying:

(1) God's intra-Trinitarian love ensures the plan of redemption. The Father so loves the Son that he has decreed that all will honour the Son even as they honour the Father. God the Father 'shows' the Son things, gives him tasks, including the supreme task of

the cross, to that end; the Son so loves the Father that out of obedience he goes to the cross on our behalf, the just for the unjust. The entire plan of redemption that has turned our hearts toward God is a function, in the first place, of this intra-Trinitarian love of God (cf. chapter 2).

(2) God's providential love protects us, feeds us, clothes us, and forbears to destroy us when mere justice could rightly write us off. The Lord Jesus insists that the evidences of God's providential love call us to faith and God-centred kingdom priorities (Matt. 6).

(3) God's yearning, inviting, commanding love, supremely displayed in the cross, 'compels us, because we are convinced that one died for all, and therefore all died. And he died for all, that those who live should no longer live for themselves but for him who died for them and was raised again' (2 Cor. 5:14–15). With Paul, we are debtors; we owe others the gospel.

(4) God's effective, electing love toward us enables us to see the sheer glory and power of Christ's vicarious death on our behalf, by which we are reconciled to God. We grasp that God has not drawn us with the savage lust of the rapist, but with the compelling wooing of the lover. Out of sheer love, God has effectively secured the salvation of his people. We love, because he first loved us.

(5) God continues to love us – not only with the immutable love that ensures we are more than conquerors through Christ who loved us (Rom. 8), but with the love of a father for his children, telling

them to remain in his love (Jude 21). Christ tells us to remain in his love by exactly the same means that he remains in his Father's love – by obedience (John 15:9ff.). Thus we are disciplined, in love, that we might be loving and obedient children of the living God.

All this has transformed us, so that we in turn perceive the sheer rightness of the first commandment – to love God with heart and soul and mind and strength. As that is the first and greatest commandment, so the first and greatest sin is *not* to love God with heart and soul and mind and strength. For this there is no remedy, save what God himself has provided – in love.

Notes

1. On distorting the love of God

1. Roy Anker, 'Not Lost in Space', *Books & Culture* 3/6 (November/December 1997), p. 13.
2. *Religious Change in America* (Cambridge: Harvard University Press, 1989), p. 37.
3. *All is forgiven: The Secular Message in American Protestantism* (Princeton: Princeton University Press, 1993).
4. Ibid., p. 40.
5. Ibid., pp. 50, 53, 135.
6. I have discussed these matters at some length in *The Gagging of God: Christianity Confronts Pluralism* (Leicester: Apollos, 1996).
7. American University Studies. Series VII: Theology and Religion, vol. 185 (New York: Peter Lang, 1996).

8. Ibid., p. 144.

9. The force of this utterance is not diminished by observing that it is addressed to the house of Israel, for not all in the house of Israel are finally saved; in Ezekiel's day, many die in judgment.

10. See Iain H. Murray, *Spurgeon and Hyper-Calvinism* (Edinburgh: Banner of Truth, 1995).

11. There are echoes as well in R. K. McGregor Wright, *No Place for Sovereignty* (Downers Grove, IL: IVP, 1996).

2. God is love

1. *Exegetical Fallacies*, 2nd edition (Grand Rapids: Baker, 1996).

2. *Agape and Eros* (New York: Harper and Row, 1969).

3. By far the most important, though certainly not the only contribution, is Robert Joly, *Le vocabulaire chrétien de l'amour est-il orginal? Philein et agapan dans le grec antique* (Brussels: Presses Universitaires, 1968).

4. *Charles Hodge, Systematic Theology*, 3 vols. (New York: Scribner, Armstrong and Co., 1972), vol. 1, pp. 428–429.

5. This view must not be confused with the claim that the Son had no pre-existence. The view described above acknowledges the pre-existence of the Son, but urges that 'the Son' as a title attaches only to his incarnational existence.

6. Because this matter is tied to debates about the roles of men and women, currently such a

delicate topic, extraordinary publications have appeared in recent years. Royce Gruenler, *The Trinity in the Gospel of John* (Grand Rapids: Baker, 1986), denies that there is any functional subordination of the Son to the Father, on the ground that each 'defers' to the other. The Father 'defers' to the Son by granting him what he asks. But this is a vain attempt to bury under the banner of deference the massive differences in the descriptions of the roles of the Father and the Son as depicted in the fourth Gospel. The fact that I 'defer' to my son's request to pick him up after the match does not mean that he commands me in the way I command him or that my love for him is displayed in obedience to him. In a recent article, Gilbert Bilezikian, 'Hermeneutical bungee-jumping: subordination in the Godhead', *Journal of the Evangelical Theological Society* 40 (1997), pp. 57–68, argues that his opponents in the debate over women's roles are flirting with heresy on this issue, since subordination in the Godhead does *not* reach back into eternity past but is restricted to the incarnation, which teaches both men and women self-denial for the sake of others. It is difficult to find many articles that so richly combine exegetical errors, historical misconceptions, and purple prose in so finely honed a synthesis. But I do utterly agree with his final appeal not to 'mess with the Trinity' in support of a contemporary agenda.

Closer to the mark is Paul K. Jewett, *God,*

Creation, and Revelation: A Neo-Evangelical
Theology (Grand Rapids: Eerdmans, 1991), pp.
322–323, who rightly concedes that the
historical view is that there is no subordination
to the Father by nature, but that there is what
many would call economic or functional
subordination. He prefers to think of it as 'the
free act of the Son'. I am not sure that this is an
adequate formulation, but even if it were, it is
difficult to imagine any complementarian
advocating something other than the free act of
the woman in any distinction in roles to which
they hold.

3. God's love and God's sovereignty

1. Wayne Grudem, *Systematic Theology: An
   Introduction to Biblical Doctrine* (Leicester: IVP,
   1994), p. 191.
2. I have dealt with such matters at greater length
   in *Divine Sovereignty and Human Responsibility*
   (Atlanta: John Knox, 1981; repr. Grand Rapids:
   Baker, 1994) and in *How Long, O Lord?
   Reflections on Suffering and Evil* (Leicester: IVP,
   1990), esp. chs. 11–12.
3. The recent attempt of John Sanders, (*The God
   Who Risks: A Theology of Providence*, Downers
   Grove, IL: IVP, 1998, pp. 103–104), to avoid
   these conclusions is remarkably unconvincing.
   He says it was God's 'definite purpose ... to
   deliver the Son into the hands of those who had
   a long track record of resisting God's work. Their

rejection did not catch God off guard, however, for he anticipated their response and so walked into the scene with an excellent prognosis ... of what would happen. The crucifixion could not have occurred to Jesus [*sic!*] unless somehow it fit into the boundaries of what God willed.' In other words, Sanders thinks the cross had a very good chance of happening: God saw there was 'an excellent prognosis' that it would all work out. Yet even he has to fudge a little by saying that 'somehow' (has mystery slipped in through the back door?) the crucifixion 'fit into the boundaries of what God willed'. Again: 'God sovereignly established limits within which humans decide how they will respond to God' – under the assumptions, in Sanders' view, of a libertarian approach to freedom. It makes more sense to adopt a straightforward reading of the text – but that means, of course, that it is essential to adopt a compatibilist understanding of freedom.

4. Herman Bavinck, *The Doctrine of God*, trans. William Hendriksen (Edinburgh: Banner of Truth, 1977 [1951]), p. 49. Cf. also discussion in Carl F. H. Henry, *God, Revelation and Authority*, vol. 5: *God Who Stands and Stays*, Part One (Wheaton, IL: Crossway Books, 1999), ch. 15.

5. Cf. Clark Pinnock, Richard Rice, John Sanders, William Hasker, David Basinger, *The Open View of God: A Biblical Challenge to the Traditional View of God* (Downers Grove, IL: IVP, 1994).

6. See the excellent essay by Millard Erickson, 'God and Change', *The Southern Baptist Journal of Theology* 1.2 (1997), pp. 38–51.

7. The most recent defence of this position is that of Peter D. Anders, 'Divine impassibility and our suffering God: how an evangelical "theology of the cross" can and *should* affirm both', *Modern Reformation* 6.4 (July/August 1997), pp. 24–30.

8. The NIV does rightly construe the Greek at this point.

4. God's love and God's wrath

1. If someone denies unconditional election, as an informed Arminian (but not an Amyraldian) would, most Calvinists would want to start further back.

2. I have defended this as the background, at some length, in my forthcoming commentary on the Johannine Epistles in the New International Greek Testament Commentary series.

3. One of the latest treatments is G. Michael Thomas, *The Extent of the Atonement: A Dilemma for Reformed Theology from Calvin to the Consensus (1536–1675)*, Paternoster Biblical and Theological Monographs (Carlisle: Paternoster, 1997).

4. Cf. somewhat similar reflections by Hywel R. Jones, 'Is God love?' in *Banner of Truth Magazine* 412 (January 1998), pp. 10–16.

5. I have dealt with this subject at much greater length in *A Call to Spiritual Reformation:*

Priorities from Paul and His Prayers (Leicester: IVP, 1992).

General index

Scripture index